THE FOUNDATIONS OF
CONSERVATIVE THOUGHT

The Foundations of Conservative Thought

An Anglo-American Tradition in Perspective

WILLIAM R. HARBOUR

UNIVERSITY OF NOTRE DAME PRESS
NOTRE DAME   LONDON

Copyright © 1982 by
University of Notre Dame Press
Notre Dame, Indiana 46556

Library of Congress Cataloging in Publication Data

Harbour, William R.
  The foundations of conservative thought.

  Bibliography: p.
  Includes index.
    1. Conservatism—United States.   2. Conservatism—
Great Britain.   3. Conservatism.   I. Title.
JA84.U5H37   1982   320.5'2   82-11011
ISBN 0-268-00959-7

Manufactured in the United States of America

This book is dedicated
to my grandparents,
BILL AND HAZEL BARRAGAR,
in recognition of
the love and care
they have given their family.

Contents

Acknowledgments

I would like to thank the following individuals who read and provided helpful criticisms of this manuscript during its development: Tim Tilton, Norm Furniss, Alan Ritter, Frank Thompson, Bill McKane, Russell Kirk, and several anonymous reviewers. I also wish to thank John Ehmann for believing in this project and his help in completing it. I am also very grateful to Pearl Agee for typing the manuscript, and I appreciate the cooperation of the staff of Lancaster Library at Longwood College.

Introduction

The purpose of our undertaking is to express and clarify the basic principles and structure of Conservative thought. Both conservative and nonconservative scholars leave unanswered too many questions about the nature and premises of Conservative thought. All too frequently one hears Conservatism defined solely in terms of support for the status quo and opposition to fundamental changes in a social system. This view would tie Conservatism to the basic forms of any social system regardless of the contents. This perception is even encouraged by those Conservatives, like Michael Oakeshott, who try to define Conservatism in terms of sentiments in favor of that which is. But this view, which deals with only one aspect of Conservative thought, leads to much confusion and leaves important questions unanswered.

The view that Conservatism simply stands for preserving any given status quo would lead to the absurd and perplexing situation in which different individuals who wish to preserve communist, liberal, conservative, and semifascist institutions in their respective countries could all be labelled as conservatives. This gross categorization would not only ignore fundamental differences among such individuals but overlook a whole body of political literature dealing with the basic principles of Conservative thought. Such an approach to the subject also makes it difficult to understand those cases where Conservatives demand changes in existing liberal policies and practices. Conceptualizing Conservatism in terms of preserving a given status quo makes it impossible to discern the real meaning of the challenge posed to American liberalism by the 1980 election of Ronald Reagan to the presidencey.

While talk of preserving social order and stability plays an important role in Conservative thought, it will be one of the purposes of this study to demonstrate that such talk only makes sense if the actual society is worth preserving. The veneration of order and stability within society will always remain superficial until one shows the value and purpose of order and until one gives substance to the kind of order that ought to be maintained. Conservatism, if it is to mean anything more than an attachment to any given status quo, must have some basic premises by which one may judge different societies. We will attempt to expose the nature of those premises.

This inquiry will also try to identify and explain Conservatism's basic philosophical orientation. In trying to clarify basic Conservative beliefs, we will emphasize the Anglo-American tradition of Conservative thought. The contributions of Continental thinkers to Conservative thought will not be ignored, but primary attention will be focused on Conservative thought in the United States and England. The reason for this decision lies in our view that the examination of basic Conservative principles can best proceed by concentrating on the more moderate Anglo-American tradition of Conservative thought as opposed to certain French and German schools of Conservative thought which often degenerate into various forms of reactionism, irrationalism, and fascism. Conservative thought greatly emphasizes notions of balance and moderation, of avoiding extremes. Conservative writers in England and the United States have had the historical advantage of being able to set forth their ideas in a more stable political and social environment. Because of this advantage they have not been forced to choose between great extremes and to overemphasize some ideas to such a degree that other basic Conservative principles are ignored. One need only compare and contrast the thought of Edmund Burke, representing English conservatism, and Joseph de Maistre, representing French conservatism, in connection with this point. For instance, both are critical of Enlightenment rationalism and wish to defend religious faith and stress the nonrational aspects of human existence. Both are critical of many of the changes taking place in Western civilization. And both wish to defend the authority of the state. But de Maistre goes far beyond Burke in his single-minded emphasis on these ideas and finally engages in the kind of theological reductionism, irrationalism, reactionism, and state-worshipping that separates his thought from the mainstream of Conservative thinking.

Continental Conservatives, because they have faced a more unstable political situation and more radical forms of class conflict and revolution, have often developed very extreme formulations of basic Conservative principles The important insights of Continental Conservatives like de Maistre into a few issues, such as the importance of authority, are purchased by neglect of other issues crucial to Conservatism, such as freedom. We believe that a more balanced and comprehensive understanding of Conservatism can be gained from concentrating on the Anglo-American tradition of Conservative thought.

Our work is not an anthology, where the reader views selections from the works of various Conservatives and is left on his own to decide what are the most important principles. Rather, there will be an attempt to explain which beliefs are most basic to Conservative thought. Not until one understands the basic philosophical orientation and underlying structure of Conservative thought is it possible to see how an individual employing Conservative principles would evaluate the culture and political institutions of different societies.

In order to understand Conservative thought adequately it is also necessary to explore the basic problems and obstacles it confronts. The difficulties facing Conservative thought are considerable and fall into two different categories. First, there are those internal tensions created by crucial ambiguities found within Conservative thought and by differing themes which can easily produce conflict. Conservative thought is very diverse, containing many bitter family quarrels. Second, there are external challenges created for Conservative thought by the philosophical, cultural, and political opposition it encounters in modern society. Any serious study of Conservative thought must consider both sets of problems.

Perhaps the first question that is asked of anyone who writes or speaks about Conservative thought is to give a simple definition of Conservatism. What is Conservatism? What does Conservatism stand for? Unfortunately, there are no simple answers to these questions. The nature and complexity of Conservative thought are such that it defies any simple analysis or definition. Much of this study is an attempt to explore the essence of Conservatism. However, it is unfair to the reader to expect that he must first read this entire book before he has any idea of what is meant by the term "Conservatism." Therefore, it is appropriate to give at least a general outline, however vague, of what we are designating as "Conservatism."

The following points are provided, not as a definitive definition of "Conservatism," but as a rough sketch of the most important beliefs found within Conservative thought:

1. Conservatism begins with a particular view of the universe and man's place in it. Conservatives generally accept what may be termed the Cosmological principle of Conservative thought. According to this principle God is at the center of all things; God is the divine ground of all existence. God, not man, is the measure of all things.

2. Man's nature is believed to be a fixed part of the Cosmological ordering of things. The Conservative holds that consideration of human nature is important to thinking about politics and that a valid political theory must be based upon an adequate account of human nature. The Conservative account of human nature stresses man's shortcomings and subordinate status within the chain of being. In contrast to the attributes he assigns to God, the Conservative perceives

man in terms of his imperfections. The Conservative believes that man's moral nature is tragically flawed and that man's greatest sin is found in his pride. And in contrast to God's perfect reason, the Conservative holds that man's reason is seriously limited when it comes to dealing with the greatest human problems.

3. Hand in hand with the Conservative's conception of human nature as a fixed part of the order of things is the belief that there is some kind of absolute moral ordering to the universe. All this leads to what may be termed theocentric humanism. Theocentric humanism is a general moral theory which views a person in spiritual terms. This theory, which constitutes the heart of the Conservative value system, is concerned with the spiritual development of the person and the cultivation of virtue.

4. From the standpoint of political theory the most important thing to note about the Conservative view of human nature is that it sets limits upon the importance and scope of politics and on what government can do about the human condition. This view of human nature, with its emphasis on the imperfectibility of man and the limitations of human reason, gives shape to one of the salient characteristics of Conservative political thought. And this is the Conservative's extremely antiutopian view of what is and is not possible in politics. The Conservative doubts the ability of man to reorganize society according to various ideal visions of what ought to be.

5. Closely associated with the Conservative's antiutopianism is the pragmatic bent in his way of thinking about politics. In evaluating different political proposals the Conservative greatly stresses the practical implications and the historical and empirical circumstances confronting the decision maker. The Conservative's belief in the limitations of human reason, in the inability of man to reorganize society according to utopian visions, and in pragmatic political thinking all lead the Conservative to reject revolution as a strategy for the grand remaking of man and society. Instead,

the Conservative favors incremental reforms when changes must be made in a society.

6.   However, while the Conservative points to the limitations of human reason when dealing with political questions, he makes considerable claims for human reason when dealing with a number of philosophical issues. The Conservative defends classical philosophy and the Judeo-Christian tradition of thought from rationalist and positivist attack. The affinity between Conservative thought and those older traditions of thought not only can be found in the importance to Conservatism of religious and metaphysical conceptions but also can be found in its general moral theory (belief in some kind of natural law). It is no small claim for human reason when the Conservative asserts that man can come to know something about an absolute moral ordering to the universe.

7.   The belief that the existence of man and society is grounded in God leads the Conservative to argue that recognition of this truth within the life of the individual and society is essential for the proper ordering of both. The Cosmological principle of Conservative thought thus leads to Conservatism's prime sociological maxim. This maxim states that religion is an essential requirement for a good society, that man is a religious being and must adopt a certain kind of religious orientation within his life if it is to be properly ordered and society made stable, morally healthy, and free.

8.   Closely tied to the Conservative's emphasis on the proper development of the person is his interest in stability within society. The Conservative veneration of order is an important part of the Conservative's theocentric humanism. Because theocentric humanism pays such attention to the spiritual life of the person, the Conservative's conception of order in society stresses the role of the religious, cultural, and intellectual environments. The Conservative argues that the key to social stability lies in the existence of long-standing, healthy customs and traditions which provide direction and meaning to the life of the individual.

9.   The importance that the Conservative attaches to order

in society forces the Conservative to be concerned with the political question of who should rule. The Conservative must show how society's political life should be organized so as to protect his basic values. There is a strong elitist orientation in the Conservative answer to the old political question of who should rule. Conservatives generally argue that only the most qualified individuals, part of a natural aristocracy, should lead a society. But such leadership must be held accountable to the people. In dealing with modern democratic politics Conservatives argue that constitutional structures should be employed to limit the power of leaders and to limit the dangers that irrational majorities pose to society. And while opposing judicial activism, they also support the rule of law and an independent judiciary as useful means of curbing what they regard as the excesses and dangers of modern democratic politics.

10. Finally, the Conservative develops a political theory which, in regard to structuring society, favors localism, small-scale social relationships, and decentralization of political institutions. The stress on localism can be found in the Conservative's veneration of the idea of community. The Conservative's stress on small-scale social relationships which permit the correct ordering and development of the individual's spiritual life goes even deeper than veneration for the idea of community. It involves veneration for the family as the most important social bond. And the Conservative's plea for decentralized political structures not only involves a defense of local government but also involves considerable apprehension over the administrative and political centralization that has characterized the development of modern nation states.

These points are not intended as part of a dogmatic definition. Any analysis of Conservative though which tries to force Conservatism into an ideological strait jacket would miss the strong antiideological cast of Conservative thinking. The student of Conservative thought confronts a significant methodological problem. One must for the sake of clarity provide an outline of the subject, which requires systematic analysis.

But Conservatism is generally critical of philosophical system building. The form of analysis may unintentionally suggest a systematic characteristic which the subject matter does not possess. The previous list of principles is not advanced as an ideological blueprint. Many individual Conservatives might wish to add to this list of principles, and some may take exception to a few of these statements. Conservatives will argue among themselves as to the proper ranking of their values and will disagree on the practical applications of their principles. One need not adhere to every idea in order to be called a Conservative. However, taken together, these ideas constitute the core meaning of Conservative thought. Explaining why this is the case is the purpose of this work.

Our examination of Conservative thought will be divided into six chapters and a conclusion. Chapter one will deal with the religious orientation of Conservative thought. While one might begin a study of Conservatism with an examination of its current political positions, such an approach would fail to put first what many Conservatives regard as an even more important element within their thinking—their underlying religious assumptions and attitudes. This approach would violate the spirit of Conservative thought and would force the analysis of it into a mold foreign to itself. Such an analysis would inhibit understanding why Conservatives are led to take certain political positions. The religious orientation of Conservative thought greatly influences the Conservative view of human nature, of man's place in the universe, of human reason, and of the limited effectiveness of politics and government in dealing with man's greatest problems. The role of religion within Conservative thought raises important questions about the relationship between faith, revelation, and reason which greatly color what Conservatives say about human reason. Religious premises fundamentally shape values central to Conservative political thought.

Chapter two of this study deals with the Conservative view of human nature. The subject of human nature falls logically between the discussion of religious orientation and an analysis of man's reason. The Conservative view of human nature owes much to certain traditional religious beliefs, and much of what the Conservative has to say about human reason is rooted in his view of human nature. And the Conservative's political theory may not be understood until one examines his conception of human nature.

Chapter three will involve an analysis of the Conservative view of human reason. It will deal with some of the basic outlooks and problems of Conservative epistemology, or theory of knowledge. In many ways understanding what is said about Conservative epistemology in this chapter will be essential to understanding the general position of Conservative thought in the modern world and the problems that Conservatism faces in an intellectual environment dominated by different epistemological theories.

Chapter four will examine Conservatism's general moral theory and its conceptualization of human freedom. Conservatism's general moral theory—its basic framework, orientation, and justification—must be explored if there is to be any understanding of the core of Conservative thought. In addition to dealing with the basic claims of Conservatism's general moral theory, this chapter will examine some of the major criticisms and problems facing that theory. The Conservative's view of human freedom will then be examined as a major extension of his general moral theory. Here one will come to see some of the major divisions that exist between different Conservative thinkers.

Chapter five will look at the Conservative discussion concerning the sources of order and disorder in the life of the individual and society. Having seen, in chapter four, which values the Conservative holds dear, this chapter will examine the way he believes society ought to be organized so as to best protect those values. What Conservative political theory says about culture, tradition, revolution, reform, political leadership, democratic politics, alienation, community, and property will all be explored in this chapter.

Chapter six will explore the relationship between theoretical and practical reason in Conservative thought. This is an important matter for Conservatism; the successful relating of the two is an important theme found in Conservative thought, and the problems that modern Conservatism has in living up to its own demand in this regard constitute one of the weaknesses of contemporary Conservatism.

In the conclusion the relationship between Conservatism and modernity will be explored. Here there will be a final attempt to clarify the meaning of Conservatism in terms of its critique of modernity. There will be a final summation of the problems and difficulties facing Conservatism and a discussion of just what Conservatism has to offer modern man.

1. The Religious Orientation of Conservatism

This inquiry into the nature of Conservatism will begin by viewing the role played by certain religious beliefs and attitudes in Conservative thinking. For one to ignore the importance of religion to Conservative thought, or to fail to deal with this subject first, would violate the spirit of Conservatism and force the analysis into a foreign mold.

PART I: THREE BASIC PRINCIPLES OF THE RELIGIOUS ORIENTATION OF CONSERVATISM

The essence of the religious orientation of Conservatism is found in the acceptance by most Conservatives of the Cosmological principle, theocentric humanism, and their chief sociological maxim. These three ideas greatly color what follows in this study of Conservative thought. They underlie much of what Conservatives say about human nature, the scope and functions of human reason, moral values, human freedom, and the sources of order and disorder in society.

Conservatism rests upon a Cosmological principle, a view of the universe and man's place in it, which is very different from the perception of the universe held by so many liberals and radicals. Conservatives by and large hold to what might be called a God-centered view of the universe, believing that

11

"God is the measure of all things." This stands in contrast to the view of many liberals and radicals in which man is alone and at the center of everything and "man is the measure of all things." Robert Nisbet, in his own discussion of the principles of Conservatism, makes a similar point. He writes:

> *First*, God and the divine order, not the natural order, must be the starting point of any understanding of society and history. What the Enlightenment and Revolution had scorned, the Conservatives sought to reestablish: the ineradicably *sacred* character of human history.[1]

This means that Conservatives oppose those who attack religious belief and try to construct their theories by considering human nature apart from man's subordinate relationship to God.

This does not mean that all Conservatives adhere to orthodox religious doctrines. Nevertheless, it is important to recall Clinton Rossiter's observation about religion being what holds Conservatism together:

> The mortar that holds together the mosaic of Conservatism is religious feeling. The first canon of Conservative thought, Russell Kirk writes, is the "belief that a divine intent rules society as well as conscience." Man is the child of God and is made in His image. Society, government, family, church—all are divine or divinely willed. Authority, liberty, morality, rights, duties—all are "strengthened with the strength of religion." "Religion," Coleridge remarked, "is and ever has been the center of gravity in a realm, to which all other things must and will accommodate themselves." From this belief Conservatism has never wandered. Those Conservatives who have doubted (and some of the greatest have fallen well short of unquestioning orthodoxy) have suppressed or surmounted their doubts in order to uphold the most powerful of conservative influences. Agnosticism is occasionally permissible,

indifference never. No conservative can afford to be casual about religion. Those political or cultural conservatives who are indifferent are to that extent—and a goodly extent it is—imperfect conservatives.[2]

An adequate analysis of Conservatism must deal with religion.

The cosmological view which stands at the beginning of Conservative thought helps to determine its estimation of the value and importance of the individual and the virtues the individual ought to cultivate. This leads Conservatism to view the individual in spiritual terms, giving primary emphasis to the health of the individual's soul or essence. Conservatism represents a particular variety of humanism.

Understanding the difference between the Conservative's humanism and cosmological perspective and the world view of the liberal and radical can best be done by reference to Jacques Maritain's distinction between "theocentric humanism" and "anthropocentric humanism." Maritain holds:

> We are thus led to distinguish between two kinds of humanism: a humanism which is theocentric or truly christian; and one which is anthropocentric, for which the spirit of the Renaissance and that of the Reformation were primarily responsible, of which we have just been speaking.
>
> The first kind of humanism recognises that the centre for man is God; it implies the christian concept of man as at once a sinner and redeemed, and the christian conception of grace and freedom, whose principles we have already called to mind. The second kind of humanism believes that man is his own centre, and therefore the centre of all things. It implies a naturalistic conception of man and of freedom.[3]

Perhaps the best conceptualization of the kind of humanism that underlies Conservative thinking is found in Dante Germino's description of "theocentric humanism" (a conceptualization that seems greatly influenced by Eric Voegelin). Germino describes "theocentric humanism" in the following fashion:

> By theocentric (literally "God-centered") humanism, I mean the conception of man found in the Western political tradition that extends from Plato ("God is the measure of all things") and Aristotle through Stoicism and Christianity. Of course, there are significant differences among Greek philosophy, Stoicism, and the Judeo-Christian tradition, but all theocentric humanists are in agreement that the divine ground of being is the source of order for men and societies, and that the good man is he whose soul is open to attunement with this world-transcendent source. The highest good (*t'agathon kai to ariston*, or *summum bonum*) is not worldly dominion, but an inward disposition that flows from the right ordering of the inclinations of the psyche. Justice or righteousness, whether for the individual or for the society, is more important than power, wealth, glory, or even fredom.[4]

This notion of "theocentric humanism" also helps to elucidate Conservatism's Cosmological principle, for it holds that the source of order in the universe is found in God. A society of human beings should manifest a law and order based on the human nature God has provided them, a human society which would reflect the order of the universe he created. The two principles are really inseparable within Conservative thought. This also helps to explain the great value that Conservatism places on the spiritual life of the individual.

The Conservative view of man's place in the universe argues against materialistic and deterministic portraits of man and society; it teaches the sacred character of human life; it opposes all the brands of collectivism which have, in this century, attempted to force the individual into compliance with various secular visions of social salvation. The struggle of a man like Alexander Solzhenitsyn against the Soviet regime has two meanings for Conservatism. First, it affirms the sanctity of the individual person against a totalitarian nation state. Second, and most importantly, Solzhenitsyn's struggle is in essence the revolt of a religious and spiritual view of man against the dominant and most radical secular ideology of the century.

The Conservative's religiously based variety of humanism accepts the ethical norms of the Judeo-Christian tradition, which serve as the moral basis of the Conservative's social criticism. It is within the context of theocentric humanism that it becomes easy to understand the basis of the Conservative's complaints about so many aspects of contemporary American society. Conservatives are increasingly critical of a society they see clearly marked by the following features: a continued decline of traditional family life and values; an epidemic of pornography which dehumanizes the relationship between man and woman and increasingly exploits children; a revolution in sexual behavior which undermines family bonds, laughs at innocence, and makes a virtue of promiscuity; the growing abuse of children; the slaughter of human life through abortions carried out on a massive scale; an increase in violent crime which reveals a political system unable to protect its citizens; and a materialistic culture which reduces human choices to a hedonistic calculus.

Because the Conservative holds that "God is the measure of all things" and that the individual and society properly order their existence by recognizing this truth, he insists on the importance of religion to social stability and the moral order. The Conservative's Cosmological principle and theocentric humanism give rise to his chief sociological maxim, which makes religion the cornerstone of the social order. Some of the key Conservative beliefs about the importance of religion to social stability are developed by Edmund Burke. Burke advances an important premise about man that has continued to serve as an underlying assumption of Conservative thought to this day when he argues that man is by nature a religious being. By this he means, first, that man's psychic health requires religious belief, that religious belief is neces-

sary for man to realize all his potential as a human being.
Second, he means that men in society must order their lives
according to certain religious principles if the society is to
be stable and a healthy environment made possible for the
individual.

Burke argues:

> We know, and it is our pride to know, that man is by his
> constitution a religious animal; that atheism is against, not
> only our reason but our instincts; and that it cannot prevail
> long. But if, in the moment of riot, and in a drunken delir-
> ium from the hot spirit drawn out of the alembick of hell,
> which France is now so furiously boiling, we should un-
> cover our madness by throwing off that Christian religion
> which has hither to been our boast and comfort, and one
> great source of civilization among us, and among many
> other nations, we are apprehensive (being well aware that
> the mind will not endure a void) that some uncouth, per-
> nicious, and degrading superstition, might take place of it.[5]

And he advances the belief that religion is an essential basis
of civil society. He states: "We know, and what is better we
feel inwardly, that religion is the basis of civil society, and the
source of all good and all comfort."[6] Burke makes repeated
use of the prime sociological maxim of Conservative thought.
This maxim holds that man is a religious being and must
adopt a proper religious orientation within his life if society
is to be stable, moral, and free. Religion is thus a prime ingre-
dient for the good society.

Because so many later Conservatives make use of this
maxim, Conservative thought has developed a very distinc-
tive and easy-to-recognize sociology. Reference to a decline
in religious belief or to a failure of the citizens to live according to certain principles of Christian ethics is almost always
a part of the explanation for internal disorder in society and
the existence of many socially unhealthy conditions. Conservative analysis of Western history since the Middle Ages
points to changes taking place within Christianity and the

changing status of Christianity vis-à-vis the rest of society. "Spiritual factors" are thus highlighted in explaining social changes.

Burke and later Conservatives treat Christianity as a chief bulwark of civilization and order in Western society. In dealing with what they fear is a dangerous decline of Christianity within modern society, they warn of two possible dangers threatening peace and stability. First, they are concerned that normlessness will replace religious beliefs. They fear that nihilism will spread through society, making a good and stable society impossible. Second, believing that man is basically a religious being, they argue that nihilism is only a temporary phenomenon and that new secular and political religions will take the place of Christianity, leading society to its destruction. Burke is fearful of what he regards as the religious zeal and dimension of the French Revolution. Perhaps the most elaborate development of the Conservative thesis that dangerous secular and political religions are responsible for the chaos and disorder found in modern history is worked out by Eric Voegelin in his study of gnosticism.[7] Conservatives argue that Nazism and Communism represent, to a considerable extent, the consequences of abandoning traditional religious restraints on human behavior and the transfer of religious passion to faith in political ideologies which promise secular salvation for man and society.

The importance of religion to Conservatives provides one useful means of distinguishing their thought from the thought of many liberals and radicals. This is not to say that there are no individuals who regard themselves as being both Conservative and agnostic or that there are not those who regard themselves as being liberal and Christian or radical and Christian. As individuals, Conservatives have no monopoly on religious beliefs. There are many theologians with liberal social views and clergy who are radical social activists. Nevertheless, the meaning of religion is different within the three modes of thought.

While Conservatism views religion in a positive light, believing it to be necessary, helpful, and liberating for man, most radicals (following Marx on this point) view religion as unnecessary, harmful, a tool of exploitation, and a sign of alienation. It is true that there are a few radicals who seek to give radicalism a theological basis. However, the theology of those radicals is fundamentally different from the theological orientation of most Conservatives. Radical theology is often gnostic in nature (meaning that the radical believes that men must be the force in history to bring about the kingdom of God on earth). The theology of many radicals who claim to believe in some kind of God is primarily a social theology.

The differences between liberals and Conservatives in regard to religion are not as great as the differences between radicals and Conservatives, but the differences are still substantial. Liberals do not go as far as radicals in criticizing religion. Those liberals who do not believe in God are usually agnostic and tolerant regarding religion. However, those radicals who do not believe in God are more likely to be atheists and active in opposing religion. Many liberals are in agreement with Conservatives on the idea that religious beliefs and practices can play a valuable and positive function in society. But liberals and Conservatives often differ in their estimation of the truth value of certain religious propositions. Many liberals perceive religious beliefs to be useful fictions that have a positive function at certain periods in history. But they also hope that the day will come when men will be "enlightened" enough for religious beliefs to no longer be necessary. On the other hand, most Conservatives not only regard the practice of religion as a social necessity but also view certain religious propositions to be true. Ultimately, most Conservatives postulate religion as a social necessity because of their own belief in a transcendental realm of existence. Because of their view of the universe and man's place in it, Conservatives are quite skeptical of liberal talk about "man's coming of age" and no longer standing in need of traditional religion.

Conservatism stresses man's dependence upon God. But liberal political thought, the offspring of the Enlightenment, emphasizes man's autonomy and reason. The social contract theory, the state of nature, naural rights, and individualism all represent a secular world view in which man is alone in the universe and is the creator of his own fate.

Most Conservatives have a view of modern secular society that is very different from that of many liberals. The majority of Conservatives, because of their prime sociological maxim, usually regard modern secularized society as disordered, morally unhealthy, and doomed in the long run. On the other hand, many liberals have either encouraged, defended, or at least been more optimistic about the prospects of a secularized society. In the course of Western history liberalism has been allied with the secularization of society while Conservatism has generally viewed the secularization of society with considerable apprehension. A revealing example of how liberals and Conservatives differ in their perception of the value and consequences of the increased secularization of society is found in the debate in the United States over the role of religion in education. The liberal, invoking a rigid wall of separation between church and state, is likely to oppose prayer and religious instruction in public schools as well as state aid to parochial schools. The Conservative, stressing the importance of religion to social order and the development of the individual, is more likely to support such policies.

It is interesting to note in connection with this point that in recent years a growing number of parents, upset with the disorders and declining academic standards of public schools, are moving their children out of public schools and into parochial schools. Conservatives are very sympathetic to what these parents are doing; they believe that a religiously based education provides a healthier environment for children. A 1980 Supreme Court decision, *Stone* v. *Graham*, which invalidated a Kentucky law requiring the placing of the Ten Commandments on each classroom wall, is symptomatic of what the Conservative believes is wrong with liberal dogma, which calls for rigid separation between church and state. The Conservative believes that children should be taught that there are moral norms, beyond the gratification of their personal desires, which everyone has an obligation to obey. Conservatives find it especially ironic that the Supreme Court decision on this matter comes at a time when violence and the lack of discipline in American public schools are increasing problems.

PART II: IMPORTANT CHARACTERISTICS OF THE
RELIGIOUS ORIENTATION OF CONSERVATISM

There are a number of important characteristics possessed by the Conservative's religious orientation which must be examined if one wishes to understand better the general structure of Conservative thought. First of all, the Conservative opposes both those who deny the truth of his religious beliefs about man and the universe and those who reduce Conservatism to religious system building. Conservatives wish to avoid both the disbelief and skepticism which they believe lead to nihilism as well as the religious certainty and dogmatism of gnosticism. Conservative thinking tends to operate in the realm of what Eric Voegelin calls "the in-between." Their religious orientation means that Conservatives believe in a divine realm of existence and try to guide their lives and thinking by their conceptions of certain transcendental truths. But also in accepting the limitations of existence in "the in-between," Conservatives realize that their contact with Being is very limited and always subject to doubt. Conservatives realize that existence in "the in-between" (between the transcendental realm of Being and nothingness) requires that special attention be paid to the everyday world about them. This means that Conservatives must give considerable weight to knowledge about this world. The balance in perspective that the Conservative seeks to maintain is in many ways very precarious. It consists of defending a view of the universe and man in which due attention must be given to a level of existence operating beyond man as well as to the problems and knowledge of the everyday world.

Conservatives face two very different sorts of opponents in trying to defend their Cosmological principle and theocentric humanism. The Conservatives must defend the Cosmological principle from those who reject it altogether on rationalistic grounds, and they must defend "the in-between" nature of Conservative belief from the irrationalist and mystic who make excessive claims for their modes of religious knowing.

On the one hand, it is important to note how the religious orientation of his thought leads the Conservative to be critical of Enlightenment philosophy and its intellectual offshoots. Indeed, many commentators on Conservative thought argue that modern Conservatism was born with the reaction against Enlightenment philosophy and the French Revolution. The Conservative distrust of Enlightenment thought begins with a defense of religion. The importance of Burke to Conservative thought on this score is considerable. Burke's counterattack on Enlightenment thought, his critique of the use of reason by Enlightenment thinkers, has become the standard Conservative critique of rationalism and occupies a central place in the development of Conservative epistemology. While later Conservatives, such as Oakeshott and Voegelin, employ greater philosophical sophistication in their attacks on rationalism, there is little in their basic critiques that was not first suggested by Burke on a polemical level. Conservatism's antirationalist position and general epistemology owe much to its religious orientation, especially to its veneration of religious and nonrationalist modes of knowing.

However, while the Conservative does oppose the type of rationalism which undercuts all religious claims, he does not turn to irrationalism in order to "save" religion. Burke's example on this score is important for the development of later Conservative thought. Burke's working within a position between Enlightenment rationalism and the reactionary thought of de Maistre sets a course for Conservatism by

which one may attack rationalism without turning to a glori-
fication of the irrational and mysterious (where only those
with special mystical knowledge are able to have any kind of
contact with truth).

In identifying important characteristics of his religious
orientation, it is not enough to simply deal with what the
Conservative opposes. One must also ask just which body of
religious beliefs Conservatives find so attractive. In asking
this question one immediately encounters an interesting and
difficult problem that concerns most Conservatives who adhere to some form of Christianity. It should not be surprising
to find that when Conservatives step down from their gen-
eralizations about the Cosmological principle and the importance of religion in order to actually reveal some of their
more specific doctrinal beliefs, most of them are attached to
certain aspects of the Christian tradition. This is especially
true of some of the outstanding Conservative thinkers of the
twentieth century: Eric Voegelin, T. S. Eliot, and C. S. Lewis.
The problem facing Conservatives involves the conflicts that
can arise when one is committed to both a defense of religion
in general and of Christianity in particular. The Conservative
who accepts Christianity faces the problem of what to say to
the advocates of other religions in non-Western parts of the
world. The Conservative faces the dilemma of having to
choose between giving primary stress and allegiance to a general belief in God's existence and a specific adherence to
Christian doctrines.

The Conservative must consider whether he is more interested in the preservation of a native religion in Africa or the
encouragement of Christianity. In the context of this dilemma
he must either back off from his own Christian beliefs or sacrifice the stability provided by an existing native religion.
Either choice is likely to damage some of his basic values.
This problem can also be seen in terms of the mixed attitude
American Conservatives must have toward the Islamic revival. On the one hand, Conservatives must sympathize a little
with the Islamic critique of the more vulgar aspects of West-

ern culture and the insistence that religion is necessary for the good society. On the other hand, anti-American sentiments and religious fanaticism must repel American Conservatives. Western Conservatives are often in an awkward position when it comes to evaluating other religious traditions.

Because of its religious orientation, Conservatism often faces the danger, through thinkers like de Maistre, of being reduced to a theological system. This danger leads some Conservative thinkers, like Oakshott, to remain silent on the question of the religious orientation of Conservative thought or to urge that the definition of Conservatism be divorced from its religious orientation. But to ignore the religious orientation of Conservatism or to try to divorce its definition from certain basic assumptions about religion would be to turn Conservatism into something which it is not. Conservative thought cannot be adequately explained without due reference to its religious dimension or to the proper recognition of the role played by its Cosmological principle, theocentric humanism, and chief sociological maxim. Yet those who insist upon preserving Conservatism's religious orientation must provide some way of showing how to prevent theological reductionism from transforming Conservatism into a religious system.

One of the sources of the reductionist danger comes from within Conservatism itself. This danger originates in the tendency of many Conservatives to engage in much loose talk about Providence. All too often individual Conservatives try to justify certain historical conditions which they approve of by simply saying that such conditions are the will of Providence. This often happens in attempts to justify certain kinds of inequalities and sometimes is even found in dubious attempts to rationalize certain forms of oppression. The problem is that there is often an unhealthy identification of the individual's will with the will of God.

However, there is a line of thought within Conservatism which warns against this danger and also protects Conservatism from the theological reductionism of the fanatic who dissolves all political and social issues down to religious terms and then reveals the will of God. While Conservatism defends the role of religion within the life of the individual and society, from Burke to Voegelin there is a strong warning against the improper mixing of religion and politics which produces the crusading mentality. Burke fears the religious fanatic who brings to politics a passionate zeal and enthusiasm. He greatly dislikes the pulpit politician; this is a dislike that contemporary Conservatives share for liberal preachers of the social gospel. Burke writes:

> No sound ought to be heard in the church but the healing voice of Christian charity. The cause of civil liberty and civil government gains little as that of religion by this confusion of duties. Those who quit their proper character, to assume what does not belong to them, are, for the greater part, ignorant both of the character they leave, and the character they assume. Wholly unacquainted with the world in which they are so fond of meddling, and inexperienced in its affairs, on which they pronounce with so much confidence, they have nothing of politics but the passions they excite. Surely the church is a place where one day's truce ought to be allowed to the dissensions and animosities of mankind.[8]

The Conservative is distrustful of those who attempt to incite religious passions in order to try to remake the world according to some divine vision; he wishes to prevent the reduction of all social and political issues to religious terms and passions. Thus, an important characteristic of Conservatism's religious dimension is that it is not all dominating and does not determine everything that is said about politics by the Conservative. While religion greatly influences the Conservative's world view, it does not dictate every specific position.

Burke's criticism of the preacher who uses his pulpit as a political platform applies not only to the liberal preacher of the social gospel and the radical priest, but it applies with equal logic to the preacher who uses his pulpit to propagandize for his right-wing political beliefs. The growth of New Right religious organizations and their impact on American politics in the late 70s and early 80s present an interesting situation to the Conservative. On the one hand, the Conservative is likely to agree with the critique of secular liberalism which many of these politically oriented fundamentalist leaders are offering. The Conservative is also likely to agree with many of the political positions taken by the fundamentalist element of the New Right. However, the Conservative must also be concerned about the impropriety of those ministers who use their pulpit as a political platform. And he must be suspicious of the extreme passions and dogmatic thinking that are often engendered by such efforts. While he rejects the secular world view of contemporary liberalism, he must also, in order to prevent the reduction of all political issues to religious issues, reject those who answer every political question with a quote from the Bible.

PART III: THE CHALLENGE TO THE CONSERVATIVE RELIGIOUS ORIENTATION

The Conservative's religious orientation faces considerable challenges and problems in modern society. In dealing with some of these problems crucial attributes of Conservatism's religious orientation can be better understood.

By far the most difficult problem Conservatism faces because of its fundamental religious orientation is that of justifying belief in its Cosmological principle. Modern Conservatism was born when great numbers of people began to doubt the truth of its Cosmological principle. One may even argue that what is generally termed "modernity" began, in a large part, when the Cosmological principle of Conservative thinking was no longer accepted as true, when it was no longer regarded as the most important of principles, by large numbers of intellectuals. As Karl Mannheim points out, this came about when the dominance of intellectual life by the priestly class was broken:

> From a sociological point of view the decisive fact of modern times, in contrast with the situation during the Middle Ages, is that this monopoly of the ecclesiastical interpretation of the world which was held by the priestly class is broken, and in the place of a closed and thoroughly organized stratum of intellectuals, a free intelligentsia has arisen. Its chief characteristic is that it is increasingly recruited from constantly varying social strata and life-situations, and that its mode of thought is no longer subject to regulation by a caste-like organization.[9]

The decline of the church's control over intellectual life in the West is characteristic of the beginning both of modernity and the assault upon the Cosmological principle within intellectual circles.

With the growing secularization of society that has accompanied the advance of modernity, the religious orientation of Conservatism appears to many either quaint (in the eyes of the kind sophisticate), a sure sign of alienation (in marxist eyes), unscientific (in the positivist manner of thinking), an ideology belonging to an earlier historical epoch (according to the sociology of knowledge advocates), not much fun (for the modern hedonist), or quite irrelevant for day-to-day living (for the average man). Conservatism finds itself in a difficult historical position. As in the case with so many of its other principles, in defending its religious orientation Conservatism must defend a position which faces increasingly powerful opposition.

The basis of the Conservative's religious orientation is the Cosmological principle. But Conservatism provides no proof, in the conventional sense of the word, for the truth of this ultimate premise. Any justification of the truth of the Cosmological principle, for the Conservative, must lie in the area of very personal, and not very communicable, life experiences. For the Conservative who is a Christian such experiences are described in terms of faith. For the Conservative with strong attachments to classical Greek philosophy, especially Plato, the experiences or means of knowing truth are described in terms of *noesis*, or intellectual apprehension.

That justifying the truth of its Cosmological principle is found in the realm of highly personal, nearly incommunicable, modes of life experiences creates much difficulty for Conservatism. Various mystics, gnostics, and irrationalists have also claimed for the truth of their beliefs a very private kind of intuitive experiences of confirmation. Yet Conservative literature has been highly critical of such mystic systems and thinkers. The Conservative must provide some means of distinguishing the experiences of faith and *noesis* from the experiences of the mystic. For the person who rejects the Cosmological principle and all talk of such things as faith and *noesis* as nonsense, the distinction between such experiences will be difficult, if not impossible, to discern.

But the Conservative can make the distinction along two different lines. First, unlike the mystic, the Conservative in accepting the Cosmological principle does not glorify the irrational. While the Conservative does admit that the Cosmological principle cannot be proven by conventional standards of proof, and that belief in it rests upon a very personal set of experiences, he will not glorify his own experiences or fall victim to the cult of the irrational. Second, the Conservative differs from the mystic in that the mystic's experiences and the truth they claim to represent give rise to a kind of certainty and dogmatism that the Conservative shuns. The Conservative accepts a degree of doubt about one's own experience and its truth. He or she does believe, but not with the same kind of obsession and certainty as the mystic. In Voegelian terms the difference between the two modes of experiences and beliefs is that the Conservative accepts his existence in "the in-between," where truth is sought and believed in, but still subject to doubt. But the mystic attempts to escape from this world altogether in an attempt to enter a dream world, where there is no doubt, only certainty.

However, for many critics of the Cosmological principle, what the Conservative calls faith or *noesis* appears as irrational as the claims made by mystics for the truth of their ecstatic experiences. For many rationalists the Conservative demonstrates his irrationality by believing something that cannot be clearly demonstrated to be true. This criticism questions basic religious beliefs about God, whose truth is to be found, according to the Conservative, either in the realm of almost incommunicable personal experiences or in the shared experiences of a special group or community (the church). Karl Mannheim's description of the basic attitude of modern rationalism explains why so many people view religious belief as irrational:

> It is the desire not to know more about things than can be expressed in a universally valid and demonstrable form, and not to incorporate them into one's experiences beyond that point. One tries to exclude from knowledge everything that is bound up with particular personalities and that can be proved only to narrow social groups with common experiences, and to confine oneself to statements which are generally communicable and demonstrable. It is therefore a desire for knowledge which can be socialized. Now quantity and calculation belong to the sphere of consciousness which is demonstrable to everyone. The new ideal of knowledge was therefore the type of proof which is found in mathematics. This meant a peculiar identification of truth with universal validity. One started out from the wholly unwarranted assumption that man can know only where he can demonstrate his experience to all. Thus, both anti-qualitative and anti-magical rationalism, from a sociological point of view, amount to a dissociation of knowledge from personalities and concrete communities,

to its being developed along wholly abstract lines (which, however, may vary among themselves).[10]

The rationalization of so many aspects of life in Western society since the decline of feudalism and the advent of the Enlightenment undermines the claims of religion and thus damages an essential dimension of Conservative thought.

The role played by rationalist and empiricist criteria of truth in the intellectual life of modern man forces the Conservative into an awkward defensive position which appears foreign and obsolete to so many intellectuals. The Conservative employs a religious principle whose truth and exact meaning appear remote and doubtful to so many individuals. The Conservative must make reference to life experiences which have little or no part in the lives of many modern people. He therefore finds it difficult, if not impossible, to communicate some of his most important beliefs to the non-Conservative.

That Conservatism provides no conventional proof for its religious claims is by no means fatal in itself. In accepting the truth of the Cosmological principle, without absolute proof, Conservatism is not the only philosophy which employs "unproven" premises or assumptions. Many political theories (such as liberalism) ultimately employ certain assumptions or basic premises (about the value of the individual or the importance of freedom) which serve as a beginning point for the rest of the theory, while the beginning point itself goes unproven. The Cosmological principle is simply such a beginning point for Conservative thought.

The real problem is not so much a matter of logic or of trying to provide conventional proof for the Cosmological principle. Rather, the crucial problem for the Conservative lies in the institutions, social structure, and way of life found in modern society. For none of these are conducive to belief in the Cosmological principle.

The chief obstacle facing the Conservative commitment to

the Cosmological principle is the limited space allowed for what some Conservatives call "the life of the spirit" in modern industrialized and secularized society. Conservatives believe that the life of the spirit is essential to the kind of life experiences which lead to a belief in the Cosmological principle. These experiences center around personal exploration of traditional religious questions and themes. This involves personal inquiry into questions about God's existence and the nature of the individual's relationship to God.

Within society at large the continued definition of the good life in terms of material accumulation, the translation of all social and political issues into economic terms, the continued emphasis on egocentric individualism, and the secularization of most aspects of life all work against the propagation of the kind of personal experiences which lead one to affirm the truth of the Cosmological principle. Most men are so occupied with different matters in their daily lives that there is little time left for the life of the spirit.

The secularization of society and the advance of secular ideologies have dealt Conservatism's religious orientation one blow after another. Historical developments in the last 200 years have increasingly put the Conservative on the defensive, often forcing Conservatives to be very pessimistic about preserving what they call "Christian civilization."

However, despite all the problems facing his religious orientation, the Conservative can still argue that acceptance of the Cosmological principle is essential for the development of theocentric humanism and that only with the acceptance of theocentric humanism by mankind will an orderly and good society be possible. The Conservative can argue that the challenges facing his religious orientation are just further signs of how bad modern society is. While he may not be able to offer conventional proof for the truth of his Cosmological principle, he can argue that acceptance of this principle and the development of theocentric humanism would be the best thing that could happen to modern society. Conservatives believe that a society in which individuals lived up to the standards of theocentric humanism would be a society in which the value and dignity of the individual would be honored and protected.

Despite all the difficulties that the Conservative faces in adhering to a way of thinking deeply influenced by religion, he is not likely to give up, no matter the number of secular critics. Believing that there is a God, that man is a religious creature who stands in need of God, and that man will always return in quest of the divine, the Conservative is much more likely to view secular society, rather than religious belief, as being doomed in the long run in the course of human development.

2. The Conservative View of Human Nature

One of the important characteristics of Conservative thought is the frequent reference made to human nature. Before going into the details of the Conservative view of human nature, one must note the significance of the belief that man even has a nature or essence. The idea that man has a nature or essence which allows us to view all persons as possessing whatever it is that constitutes a person as a person is often used in rejecting various competing political theories. Holding that there is such a thing as human nature, Conservatives assert that recognition of man's essence, or failure to make such recognition, is of important political consequence. They frequently claim that some theory or plan to reorganize society is untenable or dangerous because it "goes against human nature." This technique of dealing with certain opponents can be found in Burke, who constantly charges the Jacobins and others of working with a false conception of human nature. For Burke a valid political theory must be founded upon an accurate conception of man's nature. Burke writes, "This is the true touchstone of all theories which regard man and the affairs of men—does it suit his nature in general;—does it suit his nature as modified by his habits?"[1] For Burke a political theory which fails to have an adequate conception of human nature is bound to lead to dangerous consequences when acted upon.

PART I: ON HUMAN IMPERFECTIBILITY

The most important aspect of the Conservative view of human nature is that it implies that there are limits to what men can do politically and that man is incapable of perfection. This view of human nature, emphasizing man's imperfectibility, plays a crucial role in the antiutopian dimension of Conservative thinking (which finds expression in works like Thomas Molnar's *Utopia, The Perennial Heresy*).

It is important to note that when Conservatives speak of man being incapable of perfection, of there being limits to what man can do to improve himself, they do not mean that there are only external social circumstances, such as lack of education or economic development, that stand in the way. Rather, they argue that some real roadblocks to man's perfectibility are to be found within man himself. Conservatism thus stands opposed to the view that man is basically good but corrupted by external environment and institutions. As Peter Stanlis points out in regard to Burke's conception of human nature:

> Burke did not believe that man was instrinsically morally sound and became corrupted by the external refinements and demands of his civil institutions. Quite the reverse. To Burke the worst possible civil society was superior to any hypothetical simple "state of nature."[2]

One of Burke's earliest works, his satire *A Vindication of Natural Society*, is aimed at making fun of the view that it is society that corrupts man and that man himself is essentially good.

Conservatives hold that there is a basic flaw in man's nature which serves as the chief roadblock to man's perfectibility. Here one can see the connection between the Conservative's religious orientation and his conception of human nature. The Christian view of man, especially the idea of original sin, exercises a great influence on the Conservative view of human nature. While some Conservatives do not literally accept the Christian doctrine of original sin, most Conservatives do accept what is implied by that doctrine. They believe that the tragic course of human history testifies to man's basic moral weaknesses and shortcomings.

According to this view of the universe and man's place in it, total perfection and perfect goodness is only found in God's nature or in the realm of transcendental existence. Man exists in "the in-between" and has a nature that is mixed, containing tendencies toward both good and evil. Conservative moral theory holds that individual men should try to live their lives, as far as possible, according to the divine paradigm, but perfection itself escapes them.

This view of human nature greatly colors what Conservatives say about the scope and limitations of politics. They stand opposed to utopian thinking and radical plans to reorganize society in order to bring about a perfect realm of peace, freedom, and happiness. Because of their view of human nature, they believe such plans must fail. They doubt the efficacy of governmental policies and programs in radically improving the human condition. The Conservative does not deny that at times government is very useful. He even regards government as necessary, given man's flawed moral character. But he is generally more skeptical about what government can do to help solve man's problems than is the liberal.

One might, in connection with this point, contrast the great faith that liberals have traditionally placed in various programs for criminal rehabilitation with the skepticism Conservatives usually have regarding such efforts. Differing theories of human nature and contrasting views as to how effective government might be in altering that nature help to explain why, when dealing with the subject of crime, the liberal emphasizes altering the social conditions he believes cause crime and the importance of rehabilitation for the criminal, while the Conservative stresses the blame the criminal must bear for his acts and the need to isolate him from society.

This idea of man having a nature over which the efficacy of

government has limited access also leads the Conservative to give certain kinds of explanations for many social ills. When giving such explanations, he goes beyond mentioning various economic, social, and political institutions; he also includes his account of human nature. While he does value the contributions made by economics, sociology, psychology, and political science to understanding various social problems, he holds these explanations, by themselves, to be insufficient when it comes to viewing man's problems and predicament in their totality. As R. J. White points out:

> Conservatism sees men not under a political but under a cosmological order. Politics is therefore a means to an end beyond politics. It is not that the Conservative is more religious than other men, but that he is less confident than some other men about man's self-dependence, more inclined to mistrust the finality of man-made remedies for human ills, more prone to look for the source of these ills rather in a defective human nature than in defective laws and institutions.[3]

Conservatism insists that any discussion of the problems of human existence must give an adequate account of human nature while dealing with the contributions made by the social sciences.

Since the Conservative sees the source of many evils originating, in part, from within the nature of individual men, he disagrees with those persons who always try to rationalize or excuse individual wrongdoing by reference to the individual's social environment. He is unsympathetic toward those who blame society for their own failures or for the failures of others. He rejects the view which holds that if only society could be restructured, then individual criminal behavior would fade away. As opposed to those who emphasize man's moral failures and shortcomings as the fault of society, he emphasizes the idea of individual responsibility.

For years on American television there has appeared a public service advertisement in which a young boy is locked behind bars after stealing a car whose owner had left the keys in it. The message ends with the slogan "Don't help a good boy go bad." The Conservative, while believing the owner of the car acted foolishly, has no use for a message which places blame beyond the individual wrongdoer and doubts whether the youth in question was such a "good boy" in the first place.

However, the Conservative's emphasis on individual responsibility faces a crucial ambiguity because of his view of human nature as flawed or limited. When one reads the Conservative rejection of different doctrines of social determinism, running from Enlightenment thinkers like Helvetius to contemporaries like B. F. Skinner, one sees great emphasis on the idea of individual responsibility. Yet at certain times the Conservative's emphasis on the ideas of original sin and man's flawed or limited nature gives the impression that there is some compulsive drive inside individuals forcing them to do evil. This outlook leads to the same kind of problems faced in the history of Christian theology by those individuals who speak both of original sin and free will.

In order to get out of this problem, those Conservatives must give a more detailed explanation of what they mean when they say that man's nature is flawed or that there is a tendency toward evil in human nature. They cannot hold that man's nature is flawed in the sense that man is forced to do evil against his better intentions because of some malevolent psychic force in his will. To argue that man's nature forces him to do evil would make incoherent their view of individual responsibility.

Yet, the Conservative must assert more than the simple proposition that man's nature is flawed in the sense that man has the capacity for choosing to do evil as well as good. While such an assertion does give a very strong hint at what Conservatism has to say about human nature, in itself the assertion is inadequate because of its obvious and simple nature. Only to say that man has a capacity for choosing evil as well as good is to make no amazing discovery and keeps the discussion on a too superficial level.

In order to understand what Conservatism really means when it speaks of human nature as being flawed, it is necessary to consider a common position about human nature underlying much of liberal social reformism. This belief holds that no man really wants to do wrong. Wrongdoing is viewed as a matter of ignorance, because the person in question was never taught right from wrong, or it is viewed as a socially induced sickness which somehow forces the person to do terrible things which, if he had experienced a better social environment, he would not have done. Better education and the right kind of social engineering are seen as the means to resolving such problems. Conservatism rejects this view. Conservatism, borrowing from the Christian insight into the nature of sin, holds that a man can both know what is right in a given instance and willingly do what is wrong without being "forced" by one's environment to do so. Conservatism rejects the rationalistic view that the proper moral behavior is only a matter of the proper moral education. This rationalistic premise underlies much of the liberal's faith in education as the key to solving man's problems and creating the good society.

The Conservative view about the sources of evil in the world holds that an act of wrongdoing need not be the product of ignorance, that man, often knowing what is right, chooses to do wrong. Man is not pictured as blameless as regards evil; the Conservative does not absolve man of guilt for the existence of evil by reference to external circumstances; the origin of evil in the world is placed within man's own will.

More importantly, Conservatism holds that man may choose to do evil under ideal external circumstances, where there is no external compulsion, such as poverty or oppression, which might seem to force the individual into doing what would otherwise be regarded as wrong. Conservatives believe that the disastrous course of human history and the shortcomings within the life of every individual testify to the truth of their position.

The view that men are basically good holds that men only do wrong when they are either ignorant of what is right or when they are forced into some desperate act of wrong doing by external circumstances. Many people have great difficulty understanding how anyone would ever do wrong if only he received the proper education (to rule out ignorance), and the social, economic, and political environment were arranged so as to prevent situations in which individuals were "forced" to do what is wrong. When the Conservative denies the thesis of man's essential goodness and aserts that man's nature is flawed, he is simply holding that men can and do commit evil under the ideal circumstances which many individuals believe would assure man's proper behavior. That the source of evil in the world rests within human nature is, for the Conservative, the great roadblock to man's perfectibility.

The Conservative thus doubts the explanations of modern liberal psychology and sociology as to why men engage in immoral and destructive behavior and how such behavior can be corrected. For the Conservative views as inadequate those explanations of evil which deal only with man's environment and ignore man's nature.

PART II: MAN'S TWO NATURES AND THE PROBLEM OF DISCERNING MAN'S REAL ESSENCE

A central line of criticism directed at the Conservative view of human nature argues that the attributes assigned to human nature are really the products of man's social environment. The charge is made that Conservatives fail to see the impact of man's social environment on the life of the individual.

However, many Conservatives have gone to great lengths to show that they do not deny the tremendous influence of external social and political circumstances on the life of the individual. Burke, in speaking of the tactics and abilities of the ancient legislators, makes the following point:

They had to do with men, and they were obliged to study human nature. They had to do with citizens, and they were obliged to study the effects of those habits which are communicated by the circumstances of civil life. They were sensible that the operation of this second nature on the first produced a new calculation,—and thence arose many diversities amongst men, according to their birth, their education, their professions, and periods of their lives, their several ways of acquiring and fixing property, and according to the quality of property itself, all which rendered them, as it were, so many different species of animals.[4]

While Burke's point helps to save Conservatism from the charge that it is oblivious to the effects of society upon the life of the individual, it also complicates the Conservative view of human nature.

Burke's talk about the interaction between what he calls man's first and second natures, between his essence and what he acquires through his social environment, greatly complicates the Conservative description of the human condition. The Conservative now must speak both of man's nature and his constitution as "modified by his habits" (what Burke would call man's second nature). What this means is that Conservatism must face the possibility that many of the institutions that some individual Conservatives regard as necessary because they are founded on man's essence may derive their apparent necessity more from what Burke would call man's "second nature" than from man's real essence. All too often individual Conservatives forget this point and are guilty of simply assuming that the institutions that they approve of or are found in their own country are necessary because they are grounded in man's real essence. Here one might look at some of the Southern justifications for slavery developed prior to the Civil War.

The problem facing the Conservative is to be able to provide some way of distinguishing the institutions he believes to be based on man's essence from the institutions he holds are based on man's "second nature." The problem of making such a distinction is very great, and the Conservative's solution to the problem is seldom acceptable to others.

Once the Conservative is willing to admit that there is a kind of "second nature" to man and that it permits human institutions to take on a great variety of designs, the concept of human nature may be so watered down and made so flexible that it loses its usefulness. Alan Ryan makes the following point in connection with this problem:

> But if human nature is so manipulable, one of the functions of the notion of human nature is much impaired, for it plays a much reduced role in setting a limit to political possibility. Unless something substantial, basic, and important survives the process of socialization, and remains intact behind the social appearances, we are unable to say anything profound about how well or how ill social arrangements satisfy human needs and aspirations.[5]

It is the responsibility of the Conservative to show what it is about man's "first nature" that cannot or should not be altered by man's "second nature."

The problem facing the Conservative view of human nature, that of discovering the essence of man's nature that is supposed to lie beneath social appearances, is further complicated by Conservative talk of man being a social animal. Conservatives use Aristotle's notion of man as a social being in order to distinguish their view of man and type of social theorizing from those political theories which begin their constructions by hypothesizing isolated individuals existing in a state of nature. Thus, the Conservative distinction between man's first and second natures must be understood as an analytical distinction rather than a temporal distinction. But if Conservatism holds that man is a social being in the sense that man always exists in some kind of social environment or that man can only be understood in terms of his existence as a social being, then it becomes difficult to see how the Conservative can be confident in distinguishing between the human characteristics belonging to his underlying nature and those characteristics derived from his social relationships. If we only see men as they act in society, it then becomes difficult to tell socially induced behavior apart from what belongs to man's essence as man.

The Conservative may try to make the distinction between human characteristics which are essential to man *qua* man and those characteristics which are nonessential in several ways. But ultimately the Conservative must admit that his conception of human nature is a metaphysical conception and that one does not go about identifying and confirming the characteristics he attributes to human nature solely by ordinary scientific procedure. For this reason the distinctions that Conservatism tries to draw between man's first and second natures do not satisfy those who believe that significant statements about man must be capable of being verified solely by normal scientific standards.

One may try to argue that man's true essence can be discovered by examining all societies both past and present and seeing which characteristics man exhibits in every case. But closer analysis shows that this manner of procedure will not provide the Conservative with the kind of essentialistic characteristics which his conception of human nature requires. Even if one could overcome all the methodological difficulties involved in such a procedure and identify certain characteristics which men in all societies seem to have, there would still be no guarantee that these characteristics are not simply universal characteristics belonging to man's second nature instead of characteristics belonging to man's first nature. Such characteristics may be due to certain features found in all social structures under observation rather than traits found in what Burke calls man's first nature.

In response to this problem some Conservatives may use the idea of man being a social animal and argue that any universal characteristic that man has in all known societies is by definition a part of both man's first and second natures. While this solution to the problem has the advantage of highlighting the idea of man as a social being, it tends to collapse Burke's distinction between man's first and second natures and does considerable harm to the use which Conservatism wishes to make of the idea of human nature when attacking utopian visions of completely remaking society and man. Conservatism holds that certain basic features of human nature are such that the utopian dream of completely restructuring society so as to bring about a perfect world of peace, freedom, and happiness is a dangerous illusion. But if Conservatism defines the basic traits of human nature in terms of characteristics observed in all known societies, the utopian can still argue that his new kind of man will exist in a society entirely different from any society known to history. The utopian could then conclude that the Conservative view of human nature is really dependent upon certain kinds of societies, whereas the society the utopian has in mind will be so radically different that man's basic traits will change. For a Conservative to collapse Burke's distinction between man's first and second natures would be to undermine his view of human nature when it comes to his critique of utopian thinking and projects.

Thus, Conservatives cannot define the properties belonging to man's nature solely in terms of drawing up a list of all human traits recorded in every society. This does not mean that Conservatives close their eyes to observations about men in different societies; they regard such empirical observations about man's varying social life as very important and use such observations in a host of political arguments. They make great use of empirical knowledge about human behavior advanced by economics, psychology, sociology, anthropology, and political science. But what must be realized is that the Conservative view of human nature rests upon more than empirical descriptions of men in different societies. Ultimately the Conservative view of human nature is a metaphysical view of man, one concerned with the over-all fundamental reality of what man is. Thus, when one wishes to see how Conservatism draws the distinction between man's first and second natures in order to discover which characteristics Conservatives believe belong to man's primary essence, one must realize that a metaphysical view is being dealt with and that a metaphysical mode of reasoning is being employed. When Conservatives speak of human nature, more is involved than empirical observations from the social sciences. This becomes very clear when one examines the basic traits that they believe belong to man's essence.

PART III: THE BASIC TRAITS OF HUMAN NATURE

In reading what different Conservatives say about human nature one encounters many descriptions of human characteristics. Yet there are seven characteristics which stand out in the Conservative analysis of human nature. They are: (1) man is a religious being, (2) man's nature exists as a fixed part of the Cosmological ordering of things, (3) man's moral nature is tragically flawed, (4) there are important limits to the powers of human reason, (5) man is a social being, (6) man's greatest sin is his pride, (7) man's nature is such that moral propositions can be based upon it.

The view that man is by nature a religious being is closely connected to the Conservative's chief sociological maxim, which holds that the practice of religion is vital to a stable and healthy society. Individual Conservatives point to the practice of religion in different societies in order to illustrate the idea of man as a religious being. But while appropriate empirical evidence may be taken as a sign of man's religious nature, it hardly proves the point that the Conservative is trying to make when he says that man is a religious being. There are countless individuals who seem to practice no religion whatsoever. When the Conservative says that man is by nature a religious being, he cannot mean that all men practice religion. What is meant instead is that the practice of religion is appropriate and necessary for man's true nature and that while man can violate his nature on this point, he can do so only at the expense of his true essence—resulting in a distortion of the soul. Conservatives may point to all kinds of examples as a sign of the truth of this assumption and use their chief sociological maxim as a technique for showing what happens when man violates his true nature. For instance, the Conservative may point to individuals he knows who completely reject religion and argue that much of the unhappiness found in these individuals' lives springs from their basic rejection of what could give their lives greater meaning and purpose. But when all the empirical arguments have been reviewed, ultimately there remains the basic metaphysical assumption that man is a religious being.

What is interesting to note, in this case, is that Conservatism employs a conception of human nature which holds that man may, in a sense, violate his own nature. This also helps one to recognize the metaphysical nature of the Conservative claim, for a purely empirical interpretation of the claim would simply ask whether all men do or do not practice religion. But the metaphysical nature of the Conservative's claim permits him to explain away any example of a non-religious life by an individual as a case of an individual violating his nature. The metaphysical nature of the Conservative's claim permits him to use empirical examples which illustrate his claim and explain or put to use empirical examples which, according to an empirical interpretation of the claim, seem to refute it. Like so many metaphysical positions, the Conservative view that man is by nature a religious being contains a built-in explanation for any possible empirical example which might call the proposition into doubt.

However, this particular metaphysical claim fits well with observations about the role of religion in the course of human history. And it fits well with observations about the spiritual needs of countless individuals. One need only think of how important religion has been to the lives of millions throughout history and how religion has played a role in all different kinds of societies. While empirical observation about man's religious behavior cannot conclusively prove this metaphysical claim, such observation does add to the reasonableness of the claim. Such observations make this claim about man being a religious being far more reasonable than the contrary metaphysical claim, which holds that man by nature is a nonreligious being. It is difficult to explain the role that religion has played throughout most of human history while maintaining that religious belief is foreign to man's nature.

The metaphysical claim that man is by nature a religious being also has the advantage that it helps to support what many individuals regard as an important normative principle —the idea of religious toleration. If the religious searching of different individuals is regarded as a manifestation of man's basic nature, then one could argue that to suppress the personal religious searching or practices of any individual would be an attempt to thwart an important aspect of the individual's basic character as a human being. The Conservative claim about man's basic nature thus helps to justify an important libertarian principle.

On the other hand, if one assumes that man is basically a nonreligious being, then a violation of religious toleration may not be going against man's essential nature. Assuming that man is a nonreligious being, one might then argue that the practice of religion should be restricted so that a nonessential human activity would not be permitted to interfere with activities perceived to be more in accord with man's real nature (say, the development of man's rational faculties). Indeed, it is just such an assumption which serves as a justification for religious persecution in nations like the Soviet Union.

The second Conservative assumption about human nature, that man's nature exists as a fixed part of the Cosmological ordering of things, is clearly metaphysical in nature. Here again, in making the assertion the Conservative must rely upon some form of metaphysical intuition. This basic assumption about human nature derives ultimately from Conservatism's Cosmological principle.

The view that man's nature, like that of the entire universe, is ordered by God is one of the two great views of man and the universe. C. S. Lewis describes these two ideas in the following manner:

> Ever since men were able to think they have been wondering what this universe really is and how it came to be there. And, very roughly, two views have been held. First, there is what is called the materialist view. People who take that view think that matter and space just happen to exist, and always have existed, nobody knows why; and that the matter, behaving in certain fixed ways, has just happened, by a sort of fluke, to produce creatures like ourselves who are able to think. By one chance in a thousand something hit our sun and made it produce the planets; and by another thousandth chance the chemicals necessary for life, and the right temperature, occurred on one of these planets, and so some of the matter on this earth came alive; and then, by a long series of chances, the living creatures developed into things like us. The other view is the religious view. According to it, what is behind the universe is more like a mind than it is anything else we know. That is to say, it is conscious, and has purposes, and prefers one thing to another. And on this view it made the universe partly for purposes we do not know, but partly, at any rate, in order to produce creatures like itself—I mean, like itself to the extent of having minds. Please do not think that one of these views was held a long time ago and that the other one has gradually taken its place. Wherever there have been thinking men both views turn up. And note this too. You cannot find out which view is the right one by science in the ordinary sense.[6]

Conservatives defend what Lewis refers to as the religious view of man and the universe. While there is no final, conclusive proof for either the religious or materialist view of man and the universe, Conservatives do not dismiss the questions about man's origin and nature raised by the conflict between the two views. Unlike positivism, Conservatism regards as legitimate questions which have no clear answers in the sense of being resolved by ordinary scientific procedure. Conservatives view questions about man's origin, nature, and place in the universe as legitimate because the answers that men give to such questions can greatly affect the existential meaning they give to their lives and can influence their manner of living. The Conservative believes that his view of man and the universe assigns greater dignity and value to man than does the materialist view of man; man must deal with the ultimate questions about human existence; he believes that his view of man allows questions about the meaning and purpose of human life to be given answers which prevent the emergence of nihilism (always a danger in the materialist view of man and the universe). The Conservative believes that his view of man permits the development of theocentric humanism, whereas the materialist view of man can often lead to a lowering of human values.

The third Conservative assumption about human nature, that man's moral nature is tragically flawed, is also metaphysical in nature. Certainly Conservatives may point to many examples of evil actions in order to illustrate their point. But in the final analysis the disagreement between those who assert that man is basically good and those who claim that man's moral nature is flawed or limited is a metaphysical dispute. Each position has, within its own framework, an explanation for all the historical and empirical examples which may be used in the debate. Thus the believer in man's essential goodness can always argue that if only man's environment were completely changed in the proper way, then evil could be eliminated. Of course, this view faces the problem of explaining why a basically good creature has never managed to create such a completely changed environment. And the Conservative will always argue that the evil actions of men are, in part, reflective of a defect in man's nature and that man's moral nature will remain flawed or limited, even under ideal external circumstances. Each view depends upon some kind of metaphysical intuition concerning man's essence. However, the Conservative view more directly fits observations of human behavior.

The critic may ask the Conservative why he should even concern himself with the old question of whether man is basically good or not if the advocates of each position can simply rationalize all empirical observations in such a manner as to make safe their basic claims. However, it is possible for the Conservative to defend his asking the question of whether man is basically good or not. Any reasonable attempt to improve man's existence, to deal at least partially with the problem of evil, must at one time or another ask the question about the origin and causes of evil in the world. Solutions to various wrongs will vary greatly depending upon the analysis of their causes.

Those who accept the thesis that man is basically good and that it is man's social and economic environment that is solely to blame for acts of wrongdoing will believe that the solution to the problem of evil and unhappiness in the world is to be found through the proper restructuring of man's social environment. Such individuals will thus view the problem of evil and unhappiness primarily in political terms.

On the other hand, the Conservative does not conceptualize the problem of evil and unhappiness in the world primarily in political terms. First, the Conservative believes that much of the evil in the world is due to man's defective moral nature, not always his environment. Second, the Conservative sees much of the unhappiness in the world and much of the wrongdoing in terms of man's personal relationships with other men. The Conservative holds that to conceptualize the problem of evil solely in political terms and to lead men to believe that a political solution, the restructuring of society, holds the key to human happiness is to attach a false importance to the political realm of human existence. The Conservative holds that such a manner of thinking only raises the hopes of men in an unrealistic fashion. There remain in man's day-to-day existence all kinds of questions about personal conduct between individuals which are untouched by grand political solutions to man's problems. And it is in this area of personal relationships concerning questions of friendship, love, loyalty, and honesty where much of human happiness and unhappiness owe their source. The Conservative simply does not believe that a final solution to the problem of evil and unhappiness in the world lies in the area of political action. While he does admit to and tries to deal with various social and political evils, such evils are only viewed as a part of the human problem. The Conservative view of man's nature as flawed has the effect of diminishing the unrealistic hopes and expectations that so many individuals attach to political action.

However, while his view of human nature holds that much of human unhappiness lies beyond the realm of effective political response (and it is here where religion is so important), the Conservative does not fatalistically accept social and political evils as things about which man can do nothing. His political theory attempts to deal with such problems. But unlike the utopian, he can see no final solution to all such problems. And his view of how far government can go in altering society in order to deal with these problems is much more cautious than the view of the liberal.

The Conservative view of man's moral nature being flawed or limited also has the advantage of not facing the embarrassing problem of having to explain how man, being basically good, still winds up committing evil. For this reason the Conservative view about human nature fits easier with the fact of individual wrongdoing than does the claim that man is basically good but corrupted by warped social environments.

The fourth Conservative assumption about human nature, concerning the limitations of human reason, plays an important role in Conservative epistemology. The assumption also plays an important part in the Conservative critique of utopian thinking and in limiting the efficacy of governmental policies in dealing with man's most important problems. When the Conservative holds that human reason is basically limited, he means more than that in many given historical circumstances human reason has not been able to come up with adequate solutions to pressing problems. First, he means that human reason is only one aspect of human nature and that in many ways man is dominated by forces other than reason.

Second, even when man does turn to his reason, Conservatism holds that human reason will never, by itself, be adequate for dealing with all of the most crucial problems facing individual existence. The Conservative view of human reason is quite different from the view of human reason held by the utopian, which holds that human reason, if freed from the chains of an irrational social environment, could potentially show man how to establish the ideal community here on earth. The Conservative denies the idea of human reason having an unlimited potential.

Indeed, one of the more important developments of the last ten years has been the growing recognition in the American intellectual community that the social sciences do not, as was believed by so many liberals in the 1960s, have certain answers and solutions to all of our social problems. Increasingly one reads of former liberals who now admit the failure of so many of their programs and policies and who argue that we do not really know as much as they once thought we did. The basis of the "neoconservatism" of individuals like Irving Kristol, Norman Podhoretz, Michael Novak, and others rests, to a great extent, on the traditional Conservative conception of the limits confronting human reason. Accompanying this intellectual development has been the strong political reaction against the social engineering and expensive liberal policies left over from Lyndon Johnson's Great Society. In the immediate future liberal reform programs are likely to be subjected to much more critical scrutiny than they once were.

Conservatives can defend their view about the limits of human reason by arguing that such a view fits better with the known facts of man's irrational behavior. And the fact that so many government programs produce results quite opposite from their original intentions also points to the limits of human reason. The contrary view about human reason faces the difficult problem of explaining how human reason, being so powerful, is so often compromised by historical circumstances. Conservatives believe that the whole tragic course of human history gives weight to their contentions about the limits of human reason.

The fifth Conservative assumption about human nature, that man is a social being, holds that man is, in Aristotle's words, either a beast or a god when he stands in no need of living in a societal context. Regarding man as a social being can collapse Burke's distinction between man's first and second natures if it is misunderstood. If all the manifestations of man's social existence are considered part of what is meant by man being a social animal, then all of what is meant by man's first nature contains, by definition, all which is found in man's second nature, and Burke's distinction between the two is collapsed. Thus, Conservatism must be very careful in describing what it means when it holds that man is a social being. Conservatism must draw a distinction between its basic claim, that man's nature is such that he needs to exist in a society, and all the various manifestations of man's social existence.

The claim that man is a social being remains a metaphysical claim. For the Conservative to go beyond analysis of various manifestations of man's social existence and to postulate an underlying essence to man that requires society is to rely upon some kind of metaphysical intuition. However, while the Conservative position on this matter involves a metaphysical claim, the position is not arbitrary and can appeal to countless observations of human behavior. The claim that man is by nature a social being can draw upon psychological and sociological observations about how men develop within a social context. One need only think of the learning and development of language and how important language is to us to see how significant is our social nature. Of all the Conservative claims about human nature this is the one found most acceptable to non-Conservatives.

The sixth and seventh Conservative assumptions about human nature, that man's greatest sin is his pride and that man's nature is such that moral propositions can be based upon it, are clearly metaphysical assumptions which play an important role in Conservative moral theory. The sixth assumption contributes a significant aspect to the Conservative view of human motivation and is the reason Conservatives usually give when asked to explain just why it is that men so often choose to do what is wrong. Man's pride is believed to be the source of the tragic flaw in man's moral nature. The seventh assumption is especially crucial to Burke's natural-law position. As B. T. Wilkins points out in his study of Burke, natural-law theory depends upon the development of a conception of human nature:

> One of the basic presuppositions of natural law theory has been the belief that it is possible to talk about man and not just men. "Human nature" does not strike any natural law theorist past or present as being an unmanageable or embarrassingly vague concept. Rather such a theorist regards a discussion of human nature as being logically prior to and necessary for any worth-while account of man's natural duties and rights.[7]

The Conservative believes that political theory is impossible without some underlying conception of man's nature or essence. Questions about what man should strive to be, the structure of the good society, the meaning of justice, the distinction between political right and wrong, and how to bring about a better society can have no adequate answers until one has some ideas about what man is in the first place. The Conservative assumptions about human nature that have thus far been discussed will all have an important part in elaborating Conservative moral theory in chapter four, for one of the main uses that Conservatism does make of its view of human nature is in its moral theory.

That Conservatism even postulates such a thing as human nature supporting all aspects of human behavior does much to reveal the philosophical orientation of Conservative thought. Conservatism does not accept the positivist rule that all significant statements about man be capable of normal scientific verification. Conservatism does not reject scientific investigation and knowledge about human behavior, but it does hold that questions about man's essence are nevertheless legitimate and important areas of philosophizing. In this respect Conservatism tends to sympathize with the traditional view of what constitutes legitimate and important areas of philosophizing and distrusts modern positivist thought (which restricts the realm of philosophical inquiry).

The problem that Conservatism faces in the contemporary intellectual environment is that the modern study of man is generally oriented toward the empirical and observable dimension of human behavior. The modern social scientist believes that it is adequate simply to give an account of human behavior in terms subject to empirical verification and that to raise the metaphysical issue about man's essence is at best superfluous. The religious and intuitive elements found in the Conservative description of human nature are especially suspect. The Conservative faces the difficult task of trying to justify talking about human nature in the first place.

Conservatives can defend their concern with discerning the basic attributes of human nature by arguing along the following lines. By resolving the question "What is man?" it is easier to deal with the question of what men should do with their lives. An adequate theory of human nature would be very useful in developing a normative theory of human behavior. An adequate account of human nature could greatly add to our understanding of human needs and help solve the difficult problem of distinguishing between true and false human needs. A valid theory of human nature could help show the limits to human potential and to political action so that men would not undertake useless and unrealistic political projects. It could serve as a valuable guide for political practice. Finally, as will be shown in chapter five, the Conservative's view of human nature serves as his justification for government and as his rationale for placing constitutional constraints on those who exercise political power.

The Conservative holds that these potential benefits of being able to discern man's basic nature make inquiry into human nature a justifiable project. Unless one understands what man is, it is impossible to understand how man should live and be governed.

3. The Conservative View of Human Reason

One of the main themes found in Conservative literature concerns the proper use, scope, and limitations of human reason; as seen in their analysis of human nature, Conservatives doubt that human reason can serve as the chief tool in the realization of some utopian vision. One must deal with three basic issues concerning the Conservative view of human reason. First, there is a need for a more detailed explanation of what Conservatives mean when they speak of the inadequacies of human reason. This involves five different subjects: (1) the attack on what Burke calls "abstract speculation" or "metaphysical reasoning" in politics and what Oakeshott calls "rationalism in politics," (2) the emphasis on circumstances in political thinking—the Conservative's empirical learnings, (3) the emphasis on the proper relationship between theoretical concerns and practical political reason which comes to grips with specific historical circumstances, (4) the criticism of the rationalist mode of thought and defense of "prejudice," custom, tradition, and authority, (5) the rejection of the rationalist attack on religious faith.

After seeing the limitations that Conservatives place on human reason, the second issue concerns the claims that they make for human reason. This relates to how Conservatives claim to know that their most important beliefs are true. This deals with Conservative modes of knowing as opposed to other modes of knowing.

The third issue involves the tensions within Conservative epistemology between its empiricist, rationalist, intuitive, and traditionalist-authoritarian modes of knowing. As will be shown, there is much potential conflict between the empiricist flavoring of the Conservative's political thinking and the rationalist, intuitive, and metaphysical elements of his philosophical and religious orientation. One of the main tasks of Conservative epistomology must be to come to grips with the problems created by these conflicting themes and offer some way of reconciling them.

PART I: THE CONSERVATIVE ATTACK ON RATIONALISM

One of the central elements of Burke's political theory is his attack on the kind of reasoning used by French revolutionaries and their supporters. He argues that the Jacobins were guilty of engaging in a dangerous and fallacious kind of abstract, metaphysical political reasoning. He holds that they foolishly tried to remake the world conform to abstract blueprints of utopian dreamers. Burke feels that the abstract political reasoning which he condemns is found not only in the case of the revolutionaries but also in the case of many defenders of excessive royal powers. He argues that the French revolutionaries and the defenders of excessive royal powers (as in the case of the struggle between the American colonies and the English king) share a common error in their mode of political reasoning. In both cases Burke asserts that his opponents reason from an abstract set of principles (either the rights of man or the rights of the king or Parliament) and try to force the political world to conform rigorously to such abstract rights and powers. In each case Burke objects to the use of a geometrical mode of reasoning about politics in which certain principles are abstractly deduced and the political world then forced to conform to them. Burke is distressed by the mathematical certainty, and the desire for such certainty, characterizing the mode of reasoning which he finds in so many of his opponents. In combating those who believe that human reason can work out an absolute ethical and political system by which the lives of men and society should be ordered, Burke refers to Aristotle's warning that moral arguments could never possess geometrical accuracy. He argues that moral and political thinking cannot measure up to the standards of mathematics; such thinking requires too many exceptions; he sees prudence as the great political virtue which is to guide political thinking.[1]

Burke's attack on what he believes to be the misuse of reason by the Jacobins plays an important part in the development of the Conservative view of the scope and limitations of human reason. Many of the statements of twentieth-century Conservatives about the proper use of reason in politics can easily be traced back to what Burke says about the Jacobins. One can clearly see the parallels between Burke's attack on the Jacobins and the modern Conservative critique of the rationalist spirit in the political thought in Michael Oakeshott's famous essay "Rationalism in Politics." Oakeshott attacks the same kind of attitude about the power of human reason that Burke opposes in his critique of the Jacobin mentality. Conservatives from Burke to Oakeshott conduct a continual assault upon the political and intellectual mentality which believes that society can and should be reordered according to some kind of detailed blueprint drawn up by human reason.

Above all the Conservative doubts the claims made by partisans of the various social sciences that some new theory has been or is about to be developed which can serve as the model by which society may be explained and then reordered. The political world has too many unpredictable variables, and man's view of it is too narrow to permit the development of the kinds of general laws and formulae found in the natural sciences. Conservatives have always been skeptical of the eighteenth-century Enlightenment, nineteenth-century positivist, and twentieth-century behavioralist dreams of the social sciences being able to duplicate the successes of the natural sciences and the associated hope of then restructuring and planning society on a truly "scientific" basis. The Conservative believes that such political rationalism encompasses many "empirical theorists" who ordinarily view themselves as well removed from eighteenth-century rationalism.

Conservatives argue that the rationalist spirit in politics has as its base many of the original dispositions of Cartesian philosophy. Michael Oakeshott, in his exposition of the rationalist mentality in politics, goes to great lengths to point out the obsession of the rationalist with certainty, an obsession going back to Descartes himself.[2] The Conservative argues that the rationalist must devise absolute philosophies which explain all and must try to remake the world according to some "rational" plan because he cannot tolerate uncertainty. The conceptual and political world of the rationalist must conform to some model which measures up to Reason; all this involves a geometrical mode of reasoning so as to guarantee the certainty and purity of the model.

At the heart of this attack on the rationalist mode of thinking in politics is the insistence upon taking circumstances into account in political thinking. The notion of "circumstance" plays an important role in the Conservative's epistemology and in his rejection of a priori reasoning determining one's response to specific political issues and problems. Burke holds:

> Circumstances are infinite, are infinitely combined, are variable and transient; he who does not take them into consideration, is not erroneous, but stark mad—*dat operam ut cum ratione in saniat*—he is metaphysically mad. A statesman, never losing sight of principles, is to be guided by circumstances; and judging contrary to the exigencies of the moment, he may ruin his country for ever.[3]

It is important to note that in making this point Burke is not saying that one must abandon all thought of principles. But he is emphasizing the importance of taking circumstances into proper account:

> Circumstances (which with some gentlemen pass for nothing) give in reality to every political principle its distinguishing colour, and discriminating effect. The circumstances are what render every civil and political scheme beneficial or noxious to mankind.[4]

Conservatives, following Burke, hold that political thought must come to grips with the specific existential situations confronting men.

Conservatism holds that the circumstantial nature of the political world is such that the rationalist mentality can never successfully come to grips with it or understand it. Because the circumstances of the social and political world change in ways that cannot always be known in advance, the Conservative doubts the applicability of the rationalist's a priori mode of reasoning when one comes to working out strategies for political reform. All this emphasis on the importance of considering circumstances in thinking about specific political problems gives his political thought a strong empirical coloring. Conservatism values the inductive method when dealing with specific political problems and issues.

The Conservative's empiricist leanings greatly influence his view of the good in politics. As seen in the discussion of human nature, the Conservative is interested in general questions about the nature of the good society. But when it comes to political action such speculation about what ought to be is not allowed to blind the statesman to existing political realities and the limits of what is really possible for the political actor to change. While the Conservative believes that a wise political leader should consider theoretical questions about political right and wrong, such a leader must ultimately act in the context of a given society, within a given set of circumstances, most of which cannot be easily changed. It was in this spirit that Conservatives were so skeptical of the exaggerated promises made by Lyndon Johnson for his Great Society programs, especially for the War on Poverty. And from this framework it is easy to see why Conservatives, when it comes to American foreign policy, are so much more comfortable with the language of political realism as opposed to Wilsonian idealism. They are more comfortable with a balance of power policy toward the Soviet Union than an idealistic policy based upon good will and hopeful thinking concerning Soviet power and intentions. One need only contrast the Reagan and Carter foreign policies toward the Soviet Union in order to understand this point. And, in this context, it becomes easier to explain why the Reagan administration, soon after taking office, made it clear that while American foreign policy would still be concerned with human rights, it would carefully assess the practical implications of U.S. policy on this issue as they relate to what is really happening in the world and what can actually be changed.

Francis Canavan, in his excellent study of Burke's political thought, makes a number of points that have much bearing on Conservative thought about the nature of the political good. Of Burke's view of the political good Canavan writes:

> First, then, the political good is CONCRETE. Political reason is not concerned with the good in its abstract perfection. The object of the statesman's thought and effort is the concrete and limited good of the particular community which he has to govern, and not the good of man in the abstract.[5]

The Conservative's view of the limited and concrete nature of the political good, based upon his perception of the limited scope and power of human reason, serves as one of the chief justifications for his antiutopian and antirationalist perspectives. The political good that the Conservative seeks is a conditional good which is relative to what the circumstances permit. This is a good which fits society; it is not an abstraction for which society is turned upside down.

The Conservative's insistence upon the concrete nature of the political good and the importance of dealing with immediate circumstances in political thinking also leads to his anti-revolutionary outlook on life and his rejection of the mode of speculation and thought required for revolutionary theorizing. Karl Mannheim illustrates this point in the following manner:

> One of the most essential characteristics of this conservative way of life and thought seems to be the way in which it clings to the immediate, the actual, the *concrete*. The result is a quite new, very definite feeling for the *concrete* which is reflected in the modern use of the term "concrete" with anti-revolutionary implications. To experience and to think "concretely" now comes to mean to desire to restrict the range of one's activities to the immediate surroundings in which one is placed, and to abjure strictly all that may smack of speculation or hypothesis.[6]

This way of thinking leads to distrust of the kind of thinking about general causes and hypothesizing about how to reorganize society which is so fundamental to revolutionary thought.

All of these considerations lead Conservatives to be acutely aware of the problems in the relationship between theory and practice in political thought. Conservatism does not rule out the value and importance of theoretical reasoning, but it does insist that political thinking give proper attention to practical reasoning. As Canavan points out in regard to Burke's position on the relationship between theory and practice:

> To conclude, therefore, let us repeat that the main theme of Burke's political writings insofar as they deal with the relationship between theory and practice, is not to question the necessity or validity of theory, but to assert its insufficiency as a guide for practice. Speculative reason, Burke says, cannot furnish complete answers to practical questions. It may supply premises and principles, but these must be applied to practice by a type of reasoning which takes into account the element of the contingent and variable which is inseparable from practice. Burke therefore insists that practice must modify and correct theory: hence

the emphasis which he places on practical consequences as a criterion of the truth of theoretical speculation.[7]

Conservatism, following Burke, holds that theory and practice must interact in valid political thinking.

For Conservatism the greatest tool of human reason in dealing with the problems in the relationship between theory and practice is prudence. Prudence is supposed to be the guide by which the political leader is to mediate general principles by practical considerations in order to deal with the specific considerations of the moment. The important thing to notice about prudence is that there are no ironclad a priori rules of how it is to operate. If prudence is to be given its proper place in political thinking about specific problems, then the influence of what Burke calls "abstract speculation" must be kept under control. And it is in this area that one may find one of Burke's most important contributions to the development of Conservative thought and to political theory in general. As Leo Strauss points out:

> In opposing this intrusion of the spirit of speculation or of theory into the field of practice or of politics, Burke may be said to have restored the older view according to which theory cannot be the sole, or the sufficient guide of practice. He may be said to have returned to Aristotle in particular. But, to say nothing of other qualifications, one must add immediately that no one before Burke had spoken on this subject with equal emphasis and force. One may even say that, from the point of view of political philosophy, Burke's remarks on the problem of theory and practice are the most important part of his work. He spoke more emphatically and more forcefully on this problem than Aristotle in particular had done because he had to contend with a new and most powerful form of "speculatism" with a political doctrinairism of philosophic origin.[8]

That political thought must involve developing the proper relationship between theory and practice, with each complementing and correcting the other, is one of the basic themes of the Conservative view of the role of reason in politics.

Prudence is the key word for the Conservative whenever it comes to dealing with specific political problems. Conservatives continually emphasize their belief in prudence in dealing with specific political issues. The challenge of developing the proper relationship between theory and practice will be the central topic of concern in chapter six. There the question will be asked whether modern Conservatism has, in its politics, lived up to its own principles and satisfactorily worked out the proper relationship between theoretical and practical reasoning. This is indeed a crucial problem facing Conservative thought. Conservative epistemological principles about the role of reason in political thinking insist that "abstract speculation" be held in check and that prudence must somehow strike a balance between theoretical obligations and practical considerations. But a case can be made that, in a sense, using the Conservative's principles about reason and the nature of the world, there will always exist a fundamental tension between theory and practice and that the task of prudence may be much more difficult than some would believe. As will be shown in chapter six, one of the basic dangers confronting Conservative thought is that it faces a deep discrepancy between its theoretical and practical thought that threatens to violate its own epistemological principles about the proper use of reason in politics.

The Conservative attack on the rationalist mode of thought in politics includes much more than a criticism of the claims of the rationalist that reason can successfully remake the world after some ideal blueprint. The Conservative rejection of the rationalist view of human reason also includes a defense of "prejudice," custom, tradition, and authority against those who believe that reason must cast these aside in its pursuit of truth and in guiding the lives of men and societies.

Burke plays an important role in the history of Conservative thought on these matters. He attacks the Enlightenment and rationalist view that men should so order their lives by

pure reason that all inherited customs, tradition, and authority must be disregarded if they cannot measure up to the
dictates of reason. His defense of custom, tradition, and authority plays an important role in the Conservative view of
the scope and limitations of human reason. Burke, in making
his famous defense of "prejudice," writes:

> You see, Sir, that in this enlightened age I am bold
> enough to confess, that we are generally men of untaught
> feelings; that instead of casting away all our old prejudices,
> we cherish them to a very considerable degree, and, to take
> more shame to ourselves, we cherish them because they
> are our prejudices; and the longer they have lasted, the
> more generally they have prevailed, the more we cherish
> them. We are afraid to put men to live and trade each on
> his own private stock of reason; because we suspect that
> this stock in each man is small, and that the individuals
> would do better to avail themselves of the general bank
> and capital of nations, and of ages.[9]

The "prejudices" that Burke has in mind are beliefs and
modes of action (habits) which are handed down by custom, tradition, and religion. These "prejudices" are not the
irrational feelings and imaginations of some moment of inspiration, but instead are long established beliefs and practices. These are the beliefs and practices which have proved
meaningful over time, which have been tested by history and
embodied in tradition. "Prejudice" to Burke did not mean the
same thing that the term usually means today. As Dante
Germino points out:

> Burke did not employ "prejudice" in the wholly pejora-
> tive way in which we tend to use it today, as when we
> speak of racial or religious prejudice; to him the word
> meant rather a settled inclination or habit of mind that
> prompts the individual to respond in a predictable and
> salutary manner to a given situation without taking the
> trouble to inquire into his reasons for doing so. Prejudice

to Burke is virtuous habit; of all the prejudices of a free and rational society (for he did believe that prejudice and reason were compatible), religion was "the grand prejudice, and that which holds all other prejudice together."[10]

Conservatism holds that "prejudice" can often serve as a useful and reasonable basis of human action, whereas it would be impossible to live one's life according to the dictates of pure reason.

The Conservative holds that human reason is so limited when it comes to dealing with the complexities of life that man must often rely upon "prejudice," custom, tradition, and authority in ordering his life. He argues that it is impossible for man to live by the rationalist dictates of pure reason in which all beliefs and acts must be logically deduced as true without recourse to unproven assumptions. If each person had to logically justify every belief and action, he would be so paralyzed by an infinite regression of step-by-step analysis and demonstration that he would never be able to act. The Conservative believes that healthy traditions and customs make responsible action possible by providing the individual with a kind of moral compass. The thought and action of each individual and generation must rely upon and build from the experiences of others. And this means accepting certain things on authority from those whose previous experiences and successes merit one's trust.

The Conservative does not give so much emphasis to prejudice, custom, tradition, and authority because he wishes to glorify the irrational. He does not point out the limitations of human reason because he wishes to establish some irrational folk cult (a tendency found in fascist thought). He points to the limitations of human reason because he believes that recognizing the limitations of the rationalist mode of reasoning is a "reasonable" and necessary way of approaching life. Prejudice, custom, tradition, and authority are viewed by the Conservative not as antirational but as useful modes of living and knowing which transcend ordinary logical calculations.

They are the means of learning from others so as to expand the knowledge and capabilities of each person. They simply represent other modes of knowing how to act, as in the case of good manners and civilized behavior, which go beyond what a society of autonomous individuals could demonstrate by logical analysis. Such ways of knowing how to act, not imparted by abstract analysis, but acquired by prejudice, custom, tradition, and authority, provide the means of perpetuating the life of a civilized community.

In dealing with Burke's use of reason and defense of tradition Dante Germino makes a point that has great bearing on Conservatism's justification for believing in tradition as one possible source of truth for political reasoning:

> One detects in Burke an important anticipation of the distinction Hegel was to make between *Verstand* (understanding) and *Vernunft* (reason). Reason to Burke is not a mechanical, logic-chopping, *a priori* exercise; it is not abstract but profoundly empirical, charged with the task of discovering the innermost connections of things below the surface of mere appearance. Reason in the authentic sense is not the reverse of intuition but its self-conscious illumination. It is not in principle hostile to the traditional and venerable; rather, the ultimate rationality of many long-established institutions and practices can be amply illustrated. Like Hegel, Burke thought that reason unfolds itself in history, although by no means everything that happens in history is in accord with the law of reason.[11]

Given contemporary Conservatism's rejection of historicism, it would be dangerous to press too far the common ground that exists between the Conservative defense of tradition and the point that Germino makes about Hegel's philosophy. But what Conservatism does share with Hegel is the belief that what is traditional can also be quite reasonable. One need not hypothesize the march of Reason through history, as Hegel did, in order to see the point that Conservatives are trying to make when defending tradition as a possible source of truth in political thinking.

What Conservatism fears in the rationalist mode of thinking about politics and life in general is the attack that such a mode of thinking makes on authority and tradition (modes of thinking and living that the Conservative believes to be necessary for a satisfying life for the individual and for a stable society).

In attacking rationalism Conservatism is not attacking all forms of reasoning or advocating nihilism. The kind of reasoning which the Conservative defense of authority and tradition does stand opposed to is the kind of reasoning found in Cartesian philosophy, where nothing is accepted which cannot be deduced as absolutely certain before the judgment of the individual's private reason. As Francis Canavan points out:

> Prejudice, in the sense in which Burke praises it, is not irrational. Yet, there is a sense in which it is opposed to reason. The reason to which it is opposed is that of the thorough individualist, who is primarily concerned with his own rights and interests, who demands evidence which is clear and convincing to his mind before he will give his intellectual assent, and who acknowledges no moral law save that of his own conscience.[12]

The Conservative believes that the liberal's emphasis on the autonomous individual and the rationalist's insistence upon trying to prove everything combine to undermine the sense of authority and tradition necessary for a stable society.

Yet the liberal conception of individual autonomy and the rationalistic spirit are crucial elements of modernity. In attacking Cartesian rationalism and other forms of rationalist thought Conservatism stands opposed to one of the most basic features of modern thought—the desire to rationalize, explain, and make calculable all aspects of human existence. Reason does have a role to play in human life, as a servant of man, but not as a master or destroyer of the social bonds which make possible a civil existence.

The Conservative is critical of both the liberal conception of the autonomous individual and rationalism because together they undermine the kind of hierarchical society with all the rituals, habits, customs, and sources of authority which the Conservative believes make possible an orderly society in which each individual can understand the meaning of his life and place in society. As Leon Bramson points out, the Conservative view holds:

> Society itself exists through ritual, worship and ceremony; and without its sacred aspect, it will not hold together. Hierarchy, superordination and subordination, a definite status within the social order, are all necessary for social cohesion. Pre-rational beliefs and habits, not "reason," are the foundations of legitimate authority. Hierarchy and authority are not degrading in their effect on the individual; they reinforce consensus and protect the individual from himself. They give him a sense of place in an ordered world. Force and violence, not "irrationality" of supposedly outmoded institutions, are degrading; and they are the inevitable result of the dissolution of the normal patterns of authority.[13]

Believing that the desire to rationalize, explain, and make calculable all aspects of life damages the necessary nonrational foundations of human existence, the Conservative blames the process of rationalization, which underlies the advance of modernity, for the disorder found throughout modern society.

While the liberal is likely to see rationalism as contributing to human freedom and progress, the Conservative fears that the corrosive use of human reason is more likely to destroy the socially imposed inhibitions which hold in check the "darker" forces within man's nature. Klaus Epstein makes this point very clear in his excellent study of the origins of German Conservatism:

Conservatives assert, moreover, that man's cumulative experience with rationalism teaches that its erosion of the traditional bases of civilized conduct—religion, habit, and reverence for established custom—has unintentionally unchained primitive human drives for wealth, power, and pleasure on a scale unparalleled in history. This unintentional unleashing of drives, when combined with the pursuit of intrinsically utopian goals has made frustration and discontent the hallmark of the modern world. Even when modernity has achieved great things—as in the creation of higher living standards—the rise of expectations characteristic of the modern temper has increased faster still, the result being a net increase in dissatisfaction. The eternal facts of frustration and suffering, previously accepted as part of God's plan for maturing and regenerating man, are inexplicable to the impatient hedonism of modernity.[14]

Conservatives disagree with those who believe that a blind unleashing of human reason will make men freer and happier.

They are especially critical of the rationalist mode of thought because of its attack on religious faith. The rationalist mode of thought has been very effective in undermining various sources of religious faith, particularly in attacking the idea of authority (of the church and the gospels). Conservatism is generally skeptical of the claims made on behalf of the private judgment of individuals who use their own reason to cast aside basic doctrines of religious faith. Once one understands their belief that authority and tradition are valuable modes of knowing, it becomes easier to see why so many Conservatives appeal to the gospels and the church in explaining their religious faith.

But their critique of rationalism and defense of religion involve more. What is at stake is whether one wishes to accept faith itself as a means of encountering and knowing something, however little, about God. And here one must deal with a set of religious experiences that reveal their full meaning only to those who have them. Such an approach is, of course, completely at odds with the criteria of public, objective truth established by modern rationalism. Indeed, such experiences, as found in heretical forms of mysticism, may even pose a problem for the Conservative by challenging traditional religious beliefs and practices. The modern rationalist simply cannot accept the experiences of faith as justification for what is then believed about God. The rationalist views such experiences as too varied and the resulting beliefs as too contradictory, as witnessed by the clash of competing religious sects. But the Conservative is willing to accept the experiences of faith, especially when they are tempered by long-standing religious tradition and authority.

In explaining the differences in world view between Conservatism and liberalism it is important to recognize the debt that modern liberalism owes to rationalism. It is in the name of reason that liberals have attacked the Conservative's adherence to prejudice, custom, tradition, authority, and faith. The difference between the liberal and Conservative view of reason and authority may be seen in comparing what Immanuel Kant and C. S. Lewis have to say about Enlightenment thought and authority. Kant, speaking on behalf of Enlightenment rationalism, writes:

> Enlightenment is man's release from his self-incurred tutelage. Tutelage is man's inability to make use of his understanding without direction from another. Self-incurred is this tutelage when its cause lies not in lack of reason but in lack of resolution and courage to use it without direction from another. *Sapere aude!* "Have courage to use your own reason!"—that is the motto of enlightenment.[15]

C. S. Lewis, speaking in defense of authority, writes:

> Do not be scared by the word authority. Believing things on authority only means believing them because you have been told by someone you think trustworthy. Ninety-nine per cent of the things you believe are believed on authority. I believe there is such a place as New York. I have not seen it myself. I could not prove by abstract reasoning that there must be a place. I believe it because reliable people have

told me so. The ordinary man believes in the Solar System, atoms, evolution, and the circulation of the blood on authority—because the scientists say so. None of us has seen the Norman Conquest or the defeat of the Armada. None of us could prove them by pure logic as you would prove a thing in mathematics. We believe them simply because people who did see them left writings that tell us about them; in fact, on authority. A man who jibbed at authority in other things as some people do in religion would have to be content to know nothing all his life.[16]

Kant speaks not only on behalf of man's reason, but in particular he is expressing faith in the rationalist and liberal idea of individual autonomy. Lewis is calling into question the idea of individual autonomy and defending the idea of authority both in religion and man's day-to-day living.

Conservatives argue that reason, by itself, is not enough when it comes to influencing men to behave in a morally responsible manner; habit and custom are indispensible to decent human behavior. Lewis argues:

Let us suppose for a moment that the harder virtues could really be theoretically justified with no appeal to objective value. It still remains true that no justification of virtue will enable a man to be virtuous. Without the aid of trained emotions the intellect is powerless against the animal organism. I had sooner play cards against a man who was quite sceptical about ethics, but bred to believe that "a gentleman does not cheat," than against an irreproachable moral philosopher who had been brought up among sharpers. In battle it is not syllogisms that will keep the reluctant nerves and muscles to their post in the third hour of the bombardment.[17]

This is why Conservatives stress the individual's upbringing within a healthy set of moral and religious traditions as being more valuable to the individual than books published on ethical theory.

However, just because Conservatives reject rationalism

does not mean that they wish to be irrational or unreasonable in their respect for authority and tradition. Conservatism is often attacked because its critics believe that it entails blind acceptance of all authority and tradition, and the defense of every prejudice, as well as a refusal to employ any kind of reason in judging what has been handed down from the past. This criticism is simply not justified and confuses Conservatism with blind traditionalism and the most total form of authoritarianism. In defending authority, custom, and tradition the Conservative does not abandon the idea of reasonableness. He does not insist that any authority or tradition is as reasonable as any other tradition or that all traditions stand forever without need of prudential reform. By reasonableness he means that authority and tradition must have value for the day-to-day life of the individual. To be reasonable a tradition need not live up to any kind of scientific proof of its basic claims, but it must offer order, security, and meaning to the life of the individual.

That the Conservative believes that certain traditions should, from time to time, be modified and reformed due to historical and circumstantial changes raises a very difficult problem for Conservative thought. This problem concerns how and when a person is to know that a certain tradition stands in need of reform. Conservatives rely upon prudence to deal with this problem. But the operaton of prudence in this matter faces the problem of self-evaluation, of how to know that its suggestions for reforming a tradition will be successful if implemented. And the Conservative faces the additional problem that once he opens tradition to prudential evaluation and reform he also opens the door to further rational criticism of tradition.

PART II: THE CONSERVATIVE CLAIMS FOR HUMAN REASON

While much of their literature is dominated by comments about the limitations of human reason, Conservatives still make some substantial claims for man's reason. Despite their insistence upon prudential reasoning in solving specific political problems, they still hold that theoretical reasoning has a proper role to play in political thinking. Even Burke, who is usually used to show the empirical and pragmatic leanings of Conservative thought, argues for the importance of dealing with abstract ideas at certain times—which requires theory. Burke writes:

> I do not put abstract ideas wholly out of any question, because I well know, that under that name I should dismiss principles; and that without the guide and light of sound well-understood principles, all reasonings in politics, as in every thing else, would be only a confused jumble of particular facts and details, without the means of drawing out any sort of theoretical or practical conclusions.[18]

The Conservative recognizes that theorizing about general ideas and principles is of great importance; he just insists that theory be informed by practical considerations. Conservatives demand much of human reason when they hold that it must strike a balance between the two; they assume that human reason has sufficient scope and power to undertake such a task.

Burke makes a key statement about the value of theory which reveals many facets of Conservative thought:

> I do not vilify theory and speculation—no, because that would be to vilify reason itself. *Neque decipitur ration, neque decipit unquam.* No, whenever I speak against theory, I mean always a weak, erroneous, fallacious, unfounded, or imperfect theory; and one of the ways of discovering that it is a false theory, is by comparing it with practice. This is the true touchstone of all theories which regard man and the affairs of men—does it suit his nature in general; does it suit his nature as modified by his habits?[19]

What is important to note about this statement is the Burke

defends the role of theoretical reasoning in political thinking while linking that defense with statements of both an empirical and metaphysical nature. First of all he speaks of judging theory by comparing it with practice. Thus far it seems as though Burke is advocating some kind of empiricism. But he also introduces the idea of judging theory in light of human nature—which brings metaphysical considerations into political theorizing. In one sentence Burke manages to say that theory must consider both man's nature as modified by his habits (holding to an empiricist theme) and that theory must consider man's nature in general (holding to a metaphysical theme). That Conservatism holds that theory must deal with questions about man's essence and nature forces its epistemology to grant the possibility of human reason being able to successfully engage in such metaphysical analysis. In granting the possibility of metaphysics Conservatives are thus conceding far greater powers to human reason than would be granted by many thinkers.

Perhaps the greatest confidence that Conservatives show in the powers of human reason is found in their disposition to take seriously natural-law theory. Most Conservatives are committed to some kind of natural-law position and hold to the existence in human beings of a common nature whose genuine well-being can be expressed in a moral ordering that can be discovered by human reasoning reflecting on the human condition and human actions. While Conservatives always attack what they regard as political rationalism, there does seem to be a sense in which they are committed to a certain form of rationalism (though it is quite different from other forms of rationalism). This form of rationalism is centered on a certain view of the universe as a whole. As Francis Canavan points out:

> There is a sense, then, in which Burke can be called a political rationalist. Basically it is this, that he believed in an intelligible universal order, the product of the divine intelligence and the ruling norm for the operation of hu-

man reason in politics. All his political thought moved within the framework of a rational and moral universe. The framework constituted what we have called the metaphysical foundations of his theory of state and society.[20]

The Conservative view of natural law, which will be developed in greater detail in chapter four, makes considerable demands upon human reason; it leads Conservative epistemology to claim that the human mind can, through some form of ethical intuition or moral reasoning, come to know certain moral truths about man's natural obligations within the universal ordering of things.

In examining the religious orientation of Conservative thought one can see yet another area where Conservatives make considerable demands upon human reason. Conservatism adopts a Cosmological principle which holds that some kind of divine order holds the universe together and is the source of all existence. Conservatism holds that even practical political reason must be rooted in recognition of the Cosmological principle. Despite the Conservative's empirical and pragmatic leanings in dealing with specific political problems, underlying his thought about politics are certain metaphysical views about God, human nature, and natural law. Proper attunement to the order of being, which for Conservatism means coming to know certain truths about God, man, and the universe, as well as knowing about the existential nature of the political world, all require much of human reason.

Conservatives must place considerable faith in some form of metaphysical reasoning as a justification for many of their most important beliefs. The problem facing Conservative thought is that this process of justification is extremely vague. It is the basic vagueness of this process of metaphysical justification that renders many Conservative claims about God, human nature, and morality subject to doubt. One of the most fundamental criticisms of Conservative thought is that there has yet to appear a Conservative thinker of such magnitude, depth, and clarity who has made clear and obvious just how his basic metaphysical claims are known to be true. One can find several Conservative thinkers who perform well in elaborating basic Conservative beliefs or in showing the usefulness and importance of such beliefs, but there has yet to appear a Conservative thinker who has clearly explained the means by which such beliefs may be known to be true. In fact, Conservatives do not always agree among themselves as to how such truths are to be justified. For some the ultimate justification is by faith, for others it is by authority of the gospels and of the church, still others suggest custom and tradition, and others argue for the metaphysics of natural law. What Conservatives need to do is to provide a more detailed explication of each of these modes of knowing.

PART III: THE TENSIONS FACING THE CONSERVATIVE'S EPISTEMOLOGY

Having seen the limits that Conservatives place upon human reason, as well as the many claims that they make for human reason, it becomes apparent that there are a number of tensions existing within their epistemology created by the different themes it emphasizes. The heart of the problem lies in the fact that Conservative political thinking lays great stress on prudential thinking that deals with specific circumstances, giving Conservatism an empirical coloring, while the Conservative's philosophical and religious orientations have strong intuitive, metaphysical, and even rationalist overtones, giving Conservatism a very different epistemological orientation. Conservatism seems to limit the powers of human reason in its critique of the rationalist mode of thought and its rejection of utopian political thinking. Yet it makes considerable claims for human reason when it comes to the Conservative defense of metaphysics, religion, and natural-law theory. The contrasting themes of Conservative thought— emphasizing empirical thinking at one point; theoretical, intuitive, and metaphysical modes of thinking at other times—all make it impossible to classify Conservative epistemology along clearly defined lines of rationalism or empiricism or any other possible category. Conservative epistemology defies classification; it includes something of everything while denying the exclusive claims of any one form of knowing. Because Conservatism contains so many diverse elements and ways of knowing, it can be subjected to several criticisms challenging its internal consistency and coherence.

Some of the criticisms run along the following lines. In political thinking Conservatives are always attacking the spirit of abstract speculation, the rationalist mode of political thinking, utopian speculation, and attempts to reduce political thinking to metaphysical system-building. Yet at the same time Conservatism allows beliefs derived from intuition, metaphysical thinking, religious beliefs, and natural-law theory to greatly color what it says about politics. Despite its claims and criticisms of other modes of political thinking, Conservatism actually succumbs to political rationalism (in its dealing with natural-law theory) and abstract speculation (in its dealing with metaphysical issues and religious principles). Conservatism is to be rejected because of its superficial claim to pay attention to empirical circumstances while all along being engaged in forms of thinking which do not qualify as valid forms of scientific knowledge. Conservatism claims to reject modes of thinking which try to develop ideal models of some perfect order and then try to make the political world conform to the model. Yet it is guilty of this very thing when it takes seriously notions of natural law and the idea of there existing some kind of transcendental order of being to which men must be attuned in their daily lives. Conservatism, despite all its talk about taking circumstances into account, is really just another form of abstract speculation about politics; it represents just another form of metaphysical system-building.

The Conservative response to the above attack is twofold. Some of the criticisms simply miss the mark by misinterpreting the Conservative position, while other criticisms touch ultimate areas of disagreement where the points in dispute are so fundamental that little more can be said than that the disagreement is of such a basic nature that there is no way to resolve it.

The Conservative would reject the charge that simply because he accepts rational and metaphysical modes of thought, and views them as important, that he is guilty of political rationalism and the kind of abstract speculation and utopian thinking which seek to transform the political world so as to make it conform to some ideal model discovered by metaphysical thinking. That someone should accept metaphysical conceptions and thinking as valid does not mean that he is committed to the kind of metaphysical system-building that would characterize a Spinoza. The kind of thought that takes place in Conservative thinking about natural law is quite different from what Oakeshott and other Conservatives mean by the rationalistic mode of political thinking. The Conservative view of there being some kind of transcendental order of existence to which individuals should attune their lives is not meant to suggest a model or blueprint which government forces upon a recalcitrant society. Natural law is not an ideal to which all existence is forced to conform, but it is based on the very nature of human beings who follow its directives as experienced in the requirements and consequences of human living. The Conservative's commitment to taking circumstances into account in his political thinking is not superficial just because he also wishes to take into account considerations of metaphysical principles as well.

The most fundamental set of objections to Conservative epistemology deals with the basic questions about the validity of metaphysical and religious modes of knowing and the validity of natural-law theory. Here Conservatism is in the same position vis-a-vis positivist epistemology as is classical political philosophy. Viewed from positivist criteria, both Conservatism and classical political philosophy incorporate various truth-claims which cannot be demonstrated to be either true or false. It is no mere coincidence that so many Conservatives are found defending classical political theory and rejecting positivism. The differences between Conservative epistemology and positivism are of the most ultimate nature, each view reflecting very different ways of looking at the world and knowing about it. Conservatism, in order to justify many of its key religious and moral principles, must have recourse to faith, *noesis*, or some kind of metaphysical knowledge. Positivism rejects such modes of knowing in its attempt to describe man and his place in the world. The differences between the two are so great that there exists very little dialogue between them. Each view attacks the other view and defends itself from criticism from the other by calling upon its own dispositions and principles.

But Conservatism also faces the criticism that its epistemology, besides being vague, is simply inconsistent and incoherent. This line of criticism is made by those who demand more coherence and systematic ordering from a body of thought. At one point Conservatives speak of circumstances and practical political reasoning, and then they speak of abstract principles. They attack metaphysical system-building and then engage in metaphysical considerations. Conservatism simply fails to adopt any one mode of knowing; it has no basic epistemological model to serve as a guide in knowing.

Conservatism does have a response to such criticism. It admits that it has no one basic epistemological model. It does not attempt to set up any one mode of knowing as the only form of knowing. Its epistemology is thus pluralistic; it accepts many different modes of knowing. There is no clear-cut formula in Conservative epistemology which guides the individual in all his thinking and serves as a model for all true knowledge.

But the problem that Conservatism then faces is how to know when to employ which of its modes of knowing. Part of the Conservative answer is to rely upon the nature of the subject matter being investigated in deciding which mode of knowing to use. But this is only a partial and incomplete answer to the problem. In most matters, especially in politics, Conservatism holds that a host of different subjects have to be dealt with and that several different modes of knowing must be employed. Conservatism offers no a priori solution to the question of which mode of thought should have dominance and how to rank the different modes of knowing. Conservative thought thus appears incoherent to many.

Consider the question of what kind of foreign policy the United States should adopt in its relations with the Soviet Union. On a theoretical level Conservatives are strong anti-communists. They believe that the Soviet Union stands opposed to their most important conceptions and values. On this level of analysis the Soviet system is condemned as a major force for evil in the world. Metaphysical and ethical considerations about the place of the Soviet Union in contemporary history suggest a foreign policy based on great hostility toward the Soviet regime.

However, practical considerations, given the significant scope of Soviet military power, suggest to most Conservatives that a policy of restraining Soviet adventurism and influence is superior to a far riskier attempt to destroy the Soviet Union by military force. Thus, Conservative foreign-policy programs must rely on several modes of thinking: theoretical inquiry into the essentials of Soviet communism, empirical analysis of Soviet and American military strength, and practical evaluation of alternative courses of action. Conservatives must reject a purely theoretical approach that would base foreign policy solely on human rights as well as any policy of détente that would ignore principles.

The pluralist nature of Conservative epistemology permits great diversity, and it helps to explain many of the differences existing among individual Conservative thinkers. Some Conservatives place most of their emphasis on practical political thinking, while others concentrate on knowing certain religious and metaphysical truths. However, while individual Conservatives may differ in where they place their greatest emphasis, none of them become epistemological monists who insist that all forms of knowing be made to conform to one particular mode of knowing, or that all other modes of knowing be cast aside. And this is the most important aspect of the Conservative's view of human reason: there is no one mode of knowing that applies to all the kinds of truths which man seeks. The Conservative believes that to reduce all knowing to one simple standard would cut the individual off from many different aspects of reality. This is why he rejects the exclusive epistemological claims of rationalism, empiricism, and positivism.

Conservatism thus holds a very multifaceted view of the functioning of human reason. It believes that thinking about politics, philosophy, and religion must use reason in all its rich and various ways and that no one form of knowing ought to conquer all other forms of knowing. Just as Conservatism holds that theory and practice must interact in political thinking so as to complement and learn from each other, it also holds that all its different forms of knowing (from metaphysical reasoning, through traditionalist modes of knowing, on to empirical and practical political thinking) must be used so as to enrich each other in order to properly deal with the diverse and complex nature of man's existence. Conservatism thus tries to employ a pluralist epistemology that does justice to all aspects of the human experience, from man's practice of religion, his search for metaphysical and ethical truths, his living within inherited customs and traditions, to his practice of politics. Such a view of human reason is thus a defense of the richness and multidimensional nature of human life. This view honors man's religious experiences, his philosophical quest for metaphysical truths, his search for moral absolutes, his participation in traditions handed down from one generation to the next, and his never-ending political life.

4. The Moral Theory and Value System of Conservatism

Underlying Conservative thought is its general moral theory and value system. Part 1 of this chapter will examine the most important claims of the Conservative's moral theory, giving special attention to the internal problems facing that theory and the possible solution to those problems. Part 2 will view some of the fundamental ideas and norms which are important to his value system; it will also survey the internal tensions and problems facing that value system.

PART I: CONSERVATIVE MORAL THEORY

If one considers in isolation the Conservative's emphasis on taking circumstances into account in moral and political thinking and the stress on appreciating the different traditions and customs of individuals and societies, very wrong conclusions about his moral theory could easily result. One might surmise that his moral theory is based upon some form of ethical relativism, that he holds that right and wrong are purely relative notions that vary according to circumstance, custom, and tradition. After all, if traditions provide men with a guide for knowing how to act, and since traditions vary widely from one society to the next, how men should behave would seem to vary too. It is exactly this kind of relativism which encourages the journalistic use of the term "conservative" as a code word for those who favor the status quo in their own society, whether that society be liberal, fascist, or communist.

But such an approach to Conservatism not only clouds basic positions by lumping together political leaders of opposing social systems, it also ignores what Conservatives say in opposing moral relativism. Such an interpretation of their moral theory would entirely miss what Conservatives say about the existence of universal, absolute moral standards, of there being some kind of objective moral ordering to the universe. Despite their reference to circumstances and traditions, Conservatives are quite critical of ethical relativism.

A famous example within the history of Conservative thought in which ethical relativism is clearly rejected and an alternative moral view is advocated is found in Burke's attack on Warren Hastings in regard to misconduct in India. Burke, who elsewhere praises traditional ways of doing things, is very critical of the kind of ethical relativism that is used by one nation to justify acts of oppression in other nations. He writes:

> This geographical morality we do protest against; Mr. Hastings shall not screen himself under it. . . . We think it necessary, in justification of ourselves, to declare that the laws of morality are the same everywhere, and that there is no action which would pass for an act of extortion, of peculation, of bribery, and of oppression in England, that is not an act of extortion, of peculation, of bribery, and oppression in Europe, Asia, Africa, and all the world over. This I contend for not in the technical forms of it, but I contend for it in the substance.[1]

Circumstance and tradition do play important roles in the Conservative's thinking about moral and political issues, but he also holds that above the circumstantial and traditional level there exists an absolute moral ordering to the universe.

There is a close connection between the Conservative's

moral theory and his Cosmological principle. His belief in an objective, absolute, universal realm of values and standards of right and wrong is ultimately grounded in his belief in God and the existence of a transcendental realm of existence which serves as the ordering point of all existence. Belief in God and a transcendental realm of existence goes hand in hand with a belief in an objective moral ordering to the universe.

Because Conservatives believe in an objective moral ordering to the universe, they distrust moral and political theories which place the ultimate source of moral and political obligation in the wills of individual men. The ultimate source of moral and political authority, for Conservatives, lies outside of the wills of individual men. Burke speaks out strongly against the view that such obligations really boil down to a matter of personal choice or preference: "We have obligations to mankind at large, which are not in consequence of any special voluntary pact. They arise from the relations of man to man, and the relations of man to God, which relations are not matters of choice."[2] Burke gives an example of a set of obligations he regards as valid but not resting upon any contract or matter of choice when he speaks of the obligations of parents to their children: "Parents may not be consenting to their moral relation; but consenting or not, they are bound to a long train of burdensome duties towards those with whom they have never made a convention of any sort."[3]

Conservative moral theory, by rejecting the wills of men as the ultimate source of moral authority, greatly influences what Conservative political theory says about the sources of political obligation and rights. As Francis Canavan points out in regard to Burke's thought:

> What Burke is rejecting here is the common assumption of the political theory of his time, that the source of all authority is the wills of men. Although he by no means excludes the human will from the foundation of civil so-

ciety, he does deny that it is the source of authority and returns to the older thesis that all authority is of God.[4]

In rejecting the wills of men as the ultimate source of authority and obligation, Conservatism stands opposed to the liberal ethos that has so characterized modern thinking.

At the very heart of modern liberal political theory and thinking about the bases for moral and political rights and duties stands the social-contract theory. While there are important differences between Hobbes, Locke, Rousseau, Jefferson, Rawls, and other exponents of the social-contract theory, there is one crucial assumption they share in common. Just as moral obligations are derived from making and keeping promises, political obligations and rights spring from the idea of a social compact that men somehow enter. In each case the right thing to do and the rights men claim are derived from the wills, and thus from the desires, of men. Obligations and rights come from the agreements men make with one another. And men in turn make these agreements in pursuing their interests, in trying to satisfy their desires. Conservatives do not deny the importance of keeping promises, and they accept the value of contractual agreements relating to property. But they also adhere to a moral and political theory which places duties and rights beyond the individual preferences of men and the deals they make in trying to satisfy their desires. Conservatives believe that there are moral and political duties and rights which are valid regardless of the individual desires and contractual arrangements of autonomous individuals.

In this connection it is easy to understand the Conservatism of those critics of the women's liberation movement who argue that the "liberation of women" too frequently stresses the satisfaction of individual desires at the expense of meeting obligations to children. The Conservative believes that meeting such obligations takes moral precedence over individual career achievements. Of course, by the same logic one must also criticize those men who have, with much more social acceptance, ignored their wives and children in pursuing their own careers. Rather than urging women to imitate men in a single-minded drive for self-satisfaction, the Conservative is more likely to criticize those parents of both sexes who ignore their family obligations.

What is involved in all this is the self-seeking individualism of our contemporary culture. The liberal theory of the autonomous individual, basing obligations and rights upon the will of the individual, offers an intellectual defense for allowing the individual to do what he wants, regardless of family obligations. Thus men and women increasingly fail to meet the obligations and duties of married life, as witnessed by the divorce rate. They fail their children by neglecting them. And they abandon their own parents once they become senior citizens. So much of this is done in the pursuit of self-satisfaction for the autonomous individual. One needs to note here the cultural and moral significance of all the best-selling books written by psychologists who glorify "self-development" and explain to the thankful reader that one ought not to feel any "guilt" for "overcoming" traditional and outdated obligations. To the extent that obligations are recognized in our society, they tend to be contractual ones. Our popular psychologists, when dealing with the meeting of duties to others, stress that carrying out obligations must be rewarding to the individual—one needs to "feel good." The recipients of obligatory acts are practically forgotten in the cultivation of self-satisfaction.

All of this manifests itself politically in the tendency of so many citizens to make demands upon the state to satisfy their basic needs while at the same time denying any sense of obligation or duty to the nation. Conservatives argue that there are obligations citizens owe their countries and that citizens in Western nations have become too self-indulgent and too negligent of their civic obligations. The inability of the United States to attract enough qualified military personnel to meet all of its manpower needs is symptomatic of this problem facing Western nations whose populations enjoy a legacy of rights but have abandoned older notions of obligation.

Conservatism represents a moral and political world view which suggests that both rights and duties derive from natural laws beyond individual preferences and contractual arrangements. For Conservatism the ultimate source of all valid moral and political authority is found in a realm of absolute moral values. The Conservative is very much committed to the natural-law tradition within political theory, but his general belief in the validity of the natural-law position within political philosophy leads to a difficult problem for his moral theory. This problem grows out of the conflicting claims and implications of the natural-law themes of Conservative moral thought, which imply ethical absolutism and universalism, and the circumstantial and traditionalist themes of Conservative moral thought, which imply a certain form of ethical relativism. This crucial and difficult conflict challenges the internal coherence and consistency of Conservative moral theory.

The circumstantial and traditionalist aspects of Conservative moral thinking imply that circumstance, customs, and traditions have a great deal to do with determining what is right and wrong in differing situations and cultures. Conservatives often defend tradition as a source of moral and political truth for the individual. But all of this can frequently run counter to the natural-law themes found within Conservative moral thought. Leo Strauss, writing from the standpoint of a natural-law theorist, points out the conflict between the two themes when he writes: "If principles are sufficiently justified by the fact that they are accepted by a society, the principles of cannibalism are as defensible or sound as those of civilized life."[5] The Conservative wishes to maintain the importance of tradition as one possible source of valid moral and political thinking, while denying that a principle such as cannibalism is as valid as the traditions found in other societies.

What is involved here is a conflict between two differing

modes of thinking about morality and politics. Underlying the internal tension found within Conservative moral theory is a conflict that is found within Conservative epistemology. The natural-law approach is speculative, abstract, rationalistic, and metaphysical in nature, while the traditionalist mode of thinking is circumstantial and empirical in nature. The two styles of thinking are bound to conflict. As Leo Strauss points out:

> Yet the founders of the historical school seemed to have realized somehow that the acceptance of any universal or abstract principles has necessarily a revolutionary, disturbing, unsettling effect as far as thought is concerned and that this effect is wholly independent of whether the principles in question sanction, generally speaking, a conservative or a revolutionary course of action. For the recognition of universal principles forces man to judge the established order, or what is actual here and now, in the light of the natural or rational order; and what is actual here and now is more likely than not to fall short of the universal and unchangeable norm.[6]

If Conservative moral theory is to make any sense, it must try to show how these conflicting internal themes can be reconciled.

Conservatism has generally tried to solve the problem of reconciling these differing themes by pursuing three different lines of thought. First, there is what may be called the presumptive approach to the problem. Some Conservatives, who speak of an absolute standard of values and thus employ some form of natural-law reasoning, also operate on the basis of a presumption in favor of tradition, established institutions, customs, and moral relationships. This presumption, used by Conservatives from Edmund Burke to Russell Kirk, is the heart of the traditionalist position. For those who adhere to this position, the presumption serves as a guide to discovering what norms and practices men should live their lives by. Traditional practices are believed to be in rather close approximation to the natural law. These Conservatives argue that traditional practices must be presumed right until proven to be directly contradictory to any universal moral principle. Until proven otherwise, such practices are presumed to be validated by the course of history for having "stood the test of time."

Indeed, for this approach the best way to discover the content of natural law is carefully to examine tradition, which represents the experiences and learning of previous generations as men search for standards by which to order their lives. Here the ethical traditions found in the world's major religions come to be of crucial importance when Conservatives attempt to describe the content of the natural law.

Unfortunately for the presumptive approach, this solution to the problem of reconciling the competing themes of Conservative moral thinking would only seem to be valid under almost ideal circumstances. It would really have to be the case that a certain set of traditions comes very close to conforming to the absolute, universal standards of morality. If there were in fact no close approximation between the two, the basic presumption about their correlation could become a misleading, morally and politically disastrous assumption which would only reinforce degenerate practices and institutions. One may think here of how absurd it would be for a Conservative to argue that the Russian people ought to maintain the practices and institutions established by the Bolshevik revolution. Those Conservatives who make use of the presumptive approach to the problem always assume that their basic presumption is valid. One need only think here of how often it works out for these Conservatives that the traditions of the West are, with amazing coincidence and good fortune, in such close accord with the universal standards of morality. The problem is that the initial presumption made by those who fuse the traditionalist and natural-law positions begs the questions of those who call into doubt the relationship between the two in the first place.

That this solution to the problem is inadequate is, in a

sense, even recognized by those who propose the solution in the first place. Initial presumption about the validity of tradition is not the same as sanctifying all traditions. The position leaves the door open for a chasm between tradition and the natural law. The attempt to reconcile the traditionalist and natural-law themes of Conservative thought via the presumptive approach to the problem only works when that presumption can be proven to represent the truth about a particular society. Thus one only sees this kind of solution to the problem proposed by those who feel very happy with their society's long-established traditions and believe that they live in a society that does roughly approximate the best possible society. The individual Conservative who proposes this solution to the problem must then find himself in a relationship to his own society that is similar to the relationship that Burke had in regard to his. Such a Conservative must then exist in a kind of society that suits what Conservatives like Lord Hugh Cecil have called "natural Conservatism."

But with the advance of modernity the kind of society that Burke could feel so at home in, and in which the presumption of rough correlation between tradition and the universal rules of morality could still be made by the Conservative in good faith, has long since crumbled. The advent of the industrial order and modern rationalism, as well as the advance of modern forms of gnosticism, put an end to the social hierarchy, rural society, cultural life, and moral ethos that Conservatism values so highly. The West of the twentieth century offers little place for the kind of "natural Conservatism" which leads one to make a presumption about tradition, established institutions, and moral practices being in rough approximation to the objective moral ordering of the universe. One can seriously question the validity of that presumption in Burke's day. Although given various Conservative beliefs and the nature of Burke's society, it was at least psychologically possible to make such a presumption. However, given what twentieth-century Conservatives (like Eric Voegelin, T. S. Eliot, C. S. Lewis, and Richard Weaver) say in criticism of modern culture and civilization, it is difficult to see how a Conservative could now seriously consider such a presumption.

Those contemporary Conservatives who try to make use of such a presumption find themselves in a rather difficult and odd position. At the same time as they engage in a critique of modern values and institutions in Western society, they also speak of a presumption in favor of the traditional and established practices of that society. They must distinguish between what they regard as the "true" but ignored traditions of Western society and the modern established practices and institutions which they reject. Here the presumptive approach suffers from a divided set of traditions, institutions, and established moral practices. Older traditions are called upon in the struggle against more recently established practices. General principles of Western civilization are invoked in the campaign against contemporary trends. The very fact that the modern-day traditionalist Conservative must be so careful in picking and choosing which traditions and established practices he supports reveals the difficulty of trying to rely upon the presumptive solution in attempting to reconcile the competing themes found in Conservative moral theory.

While the presumptive solution to the problem faces a number of obstacles, there are two other possible solutions which, despite the objections raised by non-Conservatives, offer Conservatives a way to restore some kind of coherence to their moral thinking.

One of the basic themes of Conservative thought is that one ought to maintain a proper balance between theoretical and practical thinking. It is along these lines that one may find a second possible solution to the problem, which involves recognition of the problem in the first place. This approach realizes that the moral principles found in natural-law thinking are only abstract and very general guides to human action, while moral behavior on a day-to-day basis requires that one deal with circumstantial factors. All of this requires that the abstract principles be translated onto a more concrete level of existence. According to this position Conservatism is not alone in facing the problem of translating general norms and principles in such a way as to make them useful in dealing with specific moral problems. Liberals and marxists also face considerable difficulties in working out the proper relationship between their general values and practical concerns. Whereas the presumptive approach deals with the issue as a matter of somehow trying to reconcile conflicting principles, the prudential solution to the problem deals with the issue simply as a practical matter of translating general rules so as to deal with concrete situations.

Burke is aware that two different kinds of moral thinking are involved in dealing with absolute moral principles and practical political questions. What applies to one level does not always apply, in its pure form, to the other level of moral thinking. This is brought out in Burke's treatment of notions of abstract, absolute human rights:

> The pretended rights of these theorists are all extremes; and in proportion as they are metaphysically true, they are morally and politically false.[7]

For Burke the abstract rules of morality must be translated into a different form for man's day-to-day living:

> These metaphysic rights entering into common life, like rays of light which pierce into a dense medium, are, by the laws of nature, refracted from their straight line.[8]

For instance, an attempt to carry out to their logical extreme the arguments for personal freedom and contractual rights in a free-market economy could lead one to oppose restrictions on the trade of dangerous drugs. While most contemporary Conservatives defend the general principles of marketplace economics, in practice they are willing to place prudent restraints on marketplace freedoms when the circumstances are such that public safety would otherwise be endangered. Here is where the notion of prudence comes to play such an important role in Conservative moral thinking. Prudence is to serve as the means by which certain universal moral principles are translated into practical norms of conduct that allow men to deal with the circumstantial nature of their world.

Prudence also colors many aspects of the Conservative's value system. The idea of moderation becomes very important to his moral and political thinking. The emphasis on prudence and moderation helps to distinguish Conservative natural-law thought from the kind of speculation about absolute moral principles which characterizes utopian theorizing. Conservatism accepts the idea of there being an absolute moral ordering to the universe, but it also holds that it is folly to expect the empirical world to live up to the ideal. Moderation, recognition of the limits set upon moral and political perfectibility, is urged by the prudential approach. The prudential approach thus accepts the idea that there will always be a gap or tension between natural law and what is found in any one tradition. Prudence is simply supposed to come up with the best possible recommendations operable in various circumstances.

According to the prudential approach to the problem, tradition simply serves as one possible guide to the operation. Tradition is taken into consideration by prudence in dealing with the circumstantial nature of the world. This approach deals with questions of tradition as a practical matter; tradition is considered relevant to moral and political decisions because of its impact on the behavior of individuals for both good and bad.

The prudential approach to the problem, while going further in solving it than the presumptive approach, still faces some difficult questions. Of prime concern is whether or not prudence can really strike a balance between the absolute and the relative, the natural law and circumstantial aspects of Conservative moral thinking. The great challenge for the individual is in knowing whether or not one has actually struck the proper balance in his moral thinking between absolute and circumstantial considerations. Can human reason, on a prudential level, actually do what the solution requires of it? The problem is in knowing which expression of the absolute moral principles is the right expression or which is more right than the other possible expressions.

For instance, the natural-law element of Conservative thought strongly suggests that abortion is a grave moral wrong. Conservatives reject abortion for the sake of convenience. But what course of action should a couple follow when the medical circumstances are such that there is a good reason to believe that the mother will not survive pregnancy? And what if the parents already have small children who need their mother in order to have the kind of strong family upbringing Conservatives believe children need? It is much easier to perceive what is wrong in the abstract than to know how to escape from specific moral dilemmas.

The problem becomes more acute with the advance of modern society. For as modernity has advanced, the kind of absolute moral principles that Conservatism relies upon in one aspect of its moral theory become more remote, more distant, more difficult to know, understand, and prove. And tradition becomes a weaker guide to prudence in figuring out the proper translation of the transcendental norms. The traditions and customs that Conservatives rely upon in prudential moral thinking have become weak, distorted, and have often disappeared. In the context of modern society the operation of prudence becomes even more complex and difficult than in Burke's society. While the prudential solution to the problem helps to restore the internal coherence of Conservative moral theory, there remains the problem of knowing which act is the prudent act—an operational problem facing prudence that seems to grow more difficult with the advance of modernity. The very complexity of society, which grows with each step in the continuing evolution of the modern industrial order, adds considerably to the burden facing prudence when it tries to deal adequately with the circumstantial nature of man's existence.

The third possible solution to the problem of reconciling

the conflicting themes found in Conservative moral thought proceeds along lines quite different from the second approach. This third approach, which may be called the attunement approach, does not hold that the transcendental realm of values—the objective moral ordering of the universe—is of such a nature that it contains general rules of conduct which must then be translated by prudence into practical norms governing concrete moral situations. The attunement approach finds expression in Eric Voegelin's description of the idea of the Good in Platonic ethics. Voegelin writes:

> What is the Idea of the Agathon? The briefest answer to the question will best bring out the decisive point: Concerning the content of the Agathon nothing can be said at all. That is the fundamental insight of Platonic ethics. The transcendence of the Agathon makes immanent propositions concerning its content impossible. The vision of the Agathon does not render a material rule of conduct, but forms the soul through an experience of transcendence.[9]

This approach to the problem accepts the natural-law notion of there being some kind of absolute moral ordering to the universe, but it departs from many natural-law theories in that it holds that moral absolutes cannot be conceptualized in legalistic terms. This approach both upholds the idea of there being a moral ordering to the universe, which exists outside the wills of men, and suggests a way of reconciling this belief with the circumstantial themes of Conservative moral thought.

The attunement approach holds that man's inquiry into the absolute, transcendental realm of the Good has as its main object the forming of the individual's soul in such a way that the individual can then go about functioning as a moral and virtuous person. It is very important to note that this view emphasizes personal morals and conduct, not political norms. The search that takes place in ethical thought, or the attuning of the soul to the divine ground of being, is, not to discover rules of conduct, but to form the soul and ethical character of the individual so that the proper moral conduct becomes a natural part of his living. There remain absolute moral values, but according to this point of view one does not have the problem of devising the right formula and the translations of those norms. The attunement approach thus tries to by-pass subtly the problem of relating theoretical and practical moral reasoning, of translating the absolute so as to fit particular circumstances. Rather than relying on the notion of prudence to solve the problem of reconciling the conflicting themes of Conservative moral thought, this approach views the solution in terms of the right ordering of the soul— through experience with the transcendental realm of Good and the divine mind—creating the kind of virtuous man who can by-pass the difficulties found in the second solution to the problem.

However, this third approach also has its difficulties. This solution to the problem is extremely intuitive in nature; it relies upon a kind of inner knowing that is impossible to describe. Only the individual who has the experience of attunement and those individuals who have the same experience (or at least think that they have had the same experience) and so order their lives can have any confidence that it is indeed the truth by which they have ordered their moral existence. To those who have not had such an experience, the whole thing is bound to appear very suspect. There is also the additional problem of those who claim some kind of transcendental experience, but who order their lives along very different lines.

If the Conservative lived in a society where there was a common moral ethos, and if there were a commonly accepted paradigm of what constitutes the nature of the experience with the transcendent realm of the Good, and everyone knew how to recognize that experience in the moral behavior of certain men, the above problems would not appear as great as they are. However, modern man does not live in such a society, and as a result countless individuals view the attunement approach as a curious form of mysticism. The attunement approach offers a way to restore some coherence to Conservative moral thinking, reconciling some of its conflicting themes, but is not likely to make much sense to the Conservative's critics.

One wonders why Conservatives go to such lengths in defending the idea of there being some kind of objective moral ordering to the universe, considering the problem that such a view creates for the internal harmony of their moral theory. Besides believing in the existence of certain moral absolutes, Conservatives also fear what they perceive to be the consequences of moral thinking which fails to recognize the existence of such absolutes. Conservatives believe that the alternative to believing in the existence of moral absolutes is a form of relativistic moral thinking that leads ultimately to nihilism. Conservatives fear the consequences of denying the existence of an absolute moral ordering to the universe and holding that all moral principles are ultimately a matter of pure subjective choice, simply a matter of individual taste or preference. Conservatives, who greatly admire the work of Leo Strauss, agree with him when he writes:

> Once we realize that the principles of our actions have no other support than our blind choice, we really do not believe in them any more. We cannot wholeheartedly act upon them any more. We cannot live any more as responsible beings. In order to live we have to silence the easily silenced voice of reason, which tells us that our principles are in themselves as good or as bad as any other principles. The more we cultivate reason, the more we cultivate nihilism; the less we are able to be loyal members of society.[10]

They also agree with Strauss when he writes: "The contemporary rejection of natural right leads to nihilism—nay, it is identical with nihilism."[11] Nihilism runs counter to the whole Conservative conception of the universe.

Conservatism holds that an orderly and morally healthy society requires a general belief in the existence of an absolute moral ordering to the universe. Conservatives believe that relativism, in departing from that belief, is but one step on the road to nihilism and a disordered society. Conservatives are also critical of modern liberalism because they believe that it has accepted many relativistic premises which open the door to nihilism. In the Conservative's eyes modern liberals erode belief in an absolute moral ordering to the universe and help pave the way for nihilism.

The difficulty facing Conservatives is that, despite their insistence upon recognizing the existence of an absolute moral ordering to the universe, there is a problem in describing just how one is to recognize the truth of their basic moral claims.

There are a number of natural-law arguments which can be advanced in support of the Conservative's belief in the importance of freedom, order, and virtue. Man requires personal and political freedom in order to live in accordance with his own nature. Human beings have the capacity to make choices; they possess rational faculties which allow them to perceive and evaluate alternative courses of action. Nothing is more frustrating to the individual than to be forced by others to do that which his own judgment tells him is folly. Men must be free in order to satisfy the requirements of their natures.

However, as amply illustrated by the course of human history, man possesses a nature which makes him capable of great acts of cruelty to his fellow man. Because of this darker side to his nature, man needs government; public order is essential to a humane society.

The cultivation of virtue is vital to the attainment of an orderly society, and without virtue freedom becomes destructive. Man is a being who naturally makes moral distinctions. Making decisions about what is right and wrong is a mainspring to human action. The quest for virtue is necessary for the individual and society. The virtuous person is one in whom both reason and habituated inclination are disposed to do what is right. The various qualities, or virtues, of one's character help him or her to perceive the right course of action to carry out and equip one with the habits to encourage putting this perception into action.

Thus, the Conservative sees human life as dependent upon the development of freedom, order, and virtue. However, many skeptics doubt the idea that man has a nature or essence which could serve as a starting point for political thinking. Positivists question such natural-law views as violating their belief that "ought" propositions cannot be derived from "is" propositions.

The Conservative's concept of natural law is also related to a belief in the existence of a God who is the ultimate architect of man's natural obligations. But how does one prove this idea as true? Here Conservative moral theory is marred by one of the difficulties facing Conservative epistemology. The vagueness of the intuitive process by which one is to recognize the truth of the most important claims of Conservative moral theory leaves the door open to nihilism. Here one can see the precarious nature of man's existence in what Eric Voegelin calls "the in-between." The Conservative must admit that he cannot be absolutely certain of his most crucial moral claims; there is always room for doubt about his intuitive mode of knowing and the danger of a fall into nihilism. No matter how confident the Conservative may be about various moral truths, there always remains the skeptic who will demand proof for the kind of premises the Conservative takes for granted.

PART II: THE CONSERVATIVE VALUE SYSTEM

An examination of Conservative moral thinking would not be complete if it dealt only with the internal problems confronting Conservative moral theory and the difficulties of demonstrating its most basic claims. Further substance must be added to the study by viewing some of the specific norms of the Conservative value system.

The Conservative value system is centered around three key ideas: virtue, freedom, and order. The emphasis on virtue can be seen by viewing the specific content that Conservatives give to the natural law. C. S. Lewis, in his *Abolition of Man*, provides a rather detailed list of moral precepts which he believes are a part of the natural law; these precepts are drawn from the great religions of world history.[12] Two things should be noted about his collection of moral precepts. First, the precepts stress, above all else, the notion of virtue. Second, they are primarily directed at the moral behavior of the individual; they are not particularly political in their content. These points will be important to bear in mind when in chapter six the problem of relating Conservative moral principles to political questions will receive closer attention.

Given the Conservative's belief in an objective moral ordering to the universe, it should not be surprising to find virtue occupying such an important position within his value system. This value system, with its great emphasis on virtue, gives rise to a special form of humanism. Theocentric humanism, which finds its highest expression in the works of Conservatives like Eric Voegelin and C. S. Lewis, gives tremendous attention and value to the life of the individual person. It is especially concerned with what these Conservatives call "the health of the soul." The primary concern of this form of humanism is the relationship of the individual to God and the development of the moral character of the individual. The sacred character of human life and the great value that Conservatism places upon the individual are derived from the special status and quality that God has conferred upon man. The value of the individual person is seen as part of the divinely created order of things. The individual becomes sacred because of his creation in the divine image. The Conservative's theocentric humanism rests ultimately upon his Cosmological principle and view of human nature; it rests upon a picture of God at the center of all things and of man being created as an important feature in that scheme of things.

But the idea of virtue, of developing the moral character of the individual, does not stand alone at the heart of the value system which characterizes theocentric humanism. Also of crucial importance are freedom and order. Conservatives view freedom as one of their highest values, and they view a stable and orderly society as one of the greatest necessities of man's social existence. A crucial characteristic of the Conservative value system is the close connection it draws among notions of virtue, freedom, and order. The Conservative value system is pluralistic in that it views at least three values as being of the greatest importance. But the pluralism of that system is also blurred in the sense that it is difficult to tell when concern for one value ends and interest in another value begins. The Conservative holds that the three ideas are so interrelated that one ought not be so emphasized that the other two are ignored. He believes that the three concepts are so important to each other that it is difficult to speak of one without also speaking of the other two.

The close connection between the ideas of virtue, freedom, and order within this value system can be seen in statements of Burke:

> But what is liberty without wisdom, and without virtue? It is the greatest of all possible evils; for it is folly, vice, and madness, without tuition or restraint. Those who know what virtuous liberty is, cannot bear to see it disfigured by incapable heads, on account of their having high-sounding words in their mouths.[13]

> But the liberty, the only liberty I mean, is a liberty connected with order; that not only exists along with order and virtue, but which cannot exist without them. It inheres in good and steady government, as in its substance and vital principle.[14]

Virtue for the Conservative is just as important to freedom as freedom is to virtue. For Burke the question of what men do with their freedom is just as important and cannot be separated from the question of the value of their freedom in the first place. Burke is not so much concerned with any abstract definition of freedom as he is with the possible moral substance that might be given to the acts of free men. He writes:

> Is it because liberty in the abstract may be classed amongst the blessings of mankind, that I am seriously to felicitate a madman, who has escaped from the protecting restraint and wholesome darkness of his cell, on his restoration to the enjoyment of light and liberty? Am I to congratulate an highwayman and murderer, who has broken prison, upon the recovery of his natural rights?[15]

Freedom and virtue must also share their high place in the Conservative value system with order. Order is viewed as important to both freedom and virtue, and in turn the kind of order valued by the Conservative must grant plenty of room for freedom and virtue. The Conservative position on this matter may be seen in the works of contemporary Conservatives, like Russell Kirk, who continue to build upon Burke's view of a virtuous and orderly freedom. Kirk holds:

> Genuinely ordered freedom is the only sort of liberty worth having: freedom made possible by order within the soul and order within the state. Anarchic freedom, liberty defiant of authority and prescription, is merely the subhuman state of the wolf and the shark, or the punishment of Cain, with his hand against every man's.[16]

All of this means that Conservatism, even when speaking about freedom, stresses the idea of duty along with the notion of rights. Conservatism advances a view of human conduct which emphasizes the idea of accepting and acting upon extensive responsibilities. These responsibilities are not regarded as matters of pure choice, matters that can be taken up and abandoned at whim depending upon the mood of the individual. Rather, these responsibilities are set by man's relationship to God and the relationships (many of which are not voluntary) that men develop with each other in different societies. In many ways men are simply born into these relationships and the duties they entail. Conservatism distrusts talk about freedom that gives exclusive stress to notions of rights and the claims that individuals make against society while it ignores the notion of responsibility. As B. T. Wilkins points out in regard to Burke's thought:

> Burke is much impressed by man's threefold dependence upon God, the physical world, and upon other men, and he will recognize no rights (or duties) which ignore or minimize this fact of man's dependent status. Any claim to a right which encourages the alleged possessor of that right to exercise this right as though he were wholly or largely independent of other men and could safely disregard the social context upon which he depends for his very existence was anathema to Burke.[17]

Conservatism thus stands opposed to hedonistic forms of individualism; instead, it has much in common with aristocratic individualism. Part of the uneasiness that the Conservative feels toward modern Western society lies in the materialism and self-seeking that characterizes the populations of wealthy Western nations and in the associated shirking of civic duties, moral obligations, and responsibilities by so many people. Conservatives argue that many problems facing Western society are moral problems rather than political ones.

That virtue, freedom, and order are all so important within the Conservative's scheme of values creates advantages and disadvantages for his political theory. The advantage is that if he remains mindful of the close connection between the three ideas, he will be unlikely to succumb to the kind of single-minded dogmatism which so stresses one of the three that he sacrifices the other two. This is an important point to keep in mind, because it allows the observer to distinguish a true Conservative from those dogmatists on the political Right who stress one of the three values to such an extent that the other two are virtually ignored. The authoritarian sacrifices liberty to order. The anarchocaptialist sacrifices virtue and order to freedom. And the religious fanatic, who wants public law to reflect all of his values, sacrifices liberty to virtue. A true Conservative, adhering to a pluralistic value system, rejects such extremism.

However, this pluralist treatment of virtue, freedom, and order contains a certain vagueness which challenges the internal coherence of the value system, and it gives rise to considerable divisions within Conservative thought. The problem is created by the ambiguity within Conservative thought about the exact relationship between virtue, freedom, and order. This concerns just how much emphasis should be given to each of the three values. The difficult question facing every Conservative involves which value should be given greater priority in regard to different political issues. Most of the political differences existing among Conservatives touch on how to rank these values in specific instances.

The problem is manifested in the dispute among Conservatives who attach different degrees of importance to the ideas of virtue and order in relationship to human freedom. In this dispute different individuals argue for what some Conservatives call either a "traditionalist" or a "libertarian" position within Conservatism.

In giving considerable attention to this dispute, Frank Meyer held that it did not represent irreconcilable differences, but that it was simply generated by emphasizing different aspects of Conservative thought. The crucial question to ask in any analysis of the Conservative value system is whether or not Meyer was correct in holding that the two positions could be reconciled; the internal coherence of the Conservative value system rests on whether or not this is possible. Meyer's thesis is best described by his statement:

> I believe that those two streams of thought, although they are sometimes presented as mutually incompatible, can in reality be united within a single broad conservative political theory, since they have their roots in a common tradition and are arrayed against a common enemy. Their

opposition, which takes many forms, is essentially a division between those who abstract from the corpus of Western belief its stress upon freedom and upon the innate importance of the individual person (what we may call the "libertarian" position) and those who, drawing upon the same source, stress value and virtue and order (what we may call the "traditionalist" position).[18]

Before dealing with the problem of whether or not Meyer seems correct in suggesting that the two positions can be reconciled, it is important to understand why there is such a division within Conservative thought in the first place. One must ask why it is that different Conservatives are often found giving the ideas of virtue and order a very differing emphasis when relating them to the idea of human freedom.

Much of the problem derives from the influence that liberal thought has had on Conservatism. The fact that so many Conservatives have borrowed from the liberal view of freedom when it comes to discussing economic and political questions has led to a situation in which modern Conservatives have found it difficult to agree upon the exact relationship and ranking that should hold between the three values. Just how much an individual has borrowed from the classical liberal view of freedom usually determines his position in the debate between Conservatives of "traditionalist" and "libertarian" orientations.

Some Conservatives have been careful to point out that they are borrowing only certain economic and political concepts from classical liberalism and not all aspects of the philosophical underpinnings associated with liberal thought. Frank Meyer emphasizes this point when he writes:

> Granted there is much in classical liberalism that conservatism must reject—its philosophical foundations, its tendency towards Utopian constructions, its disregard (explicitly, though by no means implicitly) of tradition; granted it is the source of much that is responsible for the plight of the twentieth century; but its championship of

freedom and its development of political and economic theories directed towards the assurance of freedom have contributed to our heritage concepts which we need to conserve and develop, as surely as we need to reject the utilitarian ethics and secular progressivism that classical liberalism has also passed on to us.[19]

But those Conservatives who, like Meyer, have borrowed certain economic and political concepts from Classical liberal thought have in turn been critical of some of the political positions taken by some nineteenth-century Conservatives. These Conservatives, while respecting the general philosophical orientation of nineteenth-century Conservatives, argue that many of those Conservatives placed too much confidence and faith in the powers and authority of the state, and that what Conservatism holds to be genuine human freedom can best be protected when the state is limited in its powers and authority in some of the ways suggested by nineteenth-century liberalism. Speaking of some of the errors of nineteenth-century Conservative thinkers, Meyer writes:

> Aware, as the classical liberals were not, of the reality of original sin, they forgot that its effects are never more virulent than when men wield unlimited power. Looking to the state to promote virtue, they forgot that the power of the state rests in the hands of men as subject to the effects of original sin as those they govern.[20]

According to the view of Conservatives of "libertarian" persuasion, many nineteenth-century Conservatives gave far too much emphasis to virtue and order at the expense of freedom and were willing to place far too much power in the hands of the state. Meyer argues:

> Nineteenth-century Conservatism, with all its understanding of the pre-eminence of virtue and value, for all its piety towards the continuing tradition of mankind, was far too cavalier of the claims of freedom, far too ready to sub-

ordinate the individual person to the authority of state or society.[21]

The "libertarian" position within Conservative thought holds that in order for the value and dignity of the individual person to be protected, one must always remember the dangers that excessive state powers pose to the individual. The crucial part of the classical liberal view of freedom which these Conservatives adopt is the idea that the essential part of human freedom involves being free from coercion and that it is the coercive powers of the state which must be kept under control. For this reason Meyer criticizes many nineteenth-century Conservatives because:

> Sound though they were on the essentials of man's being, on his destiny to virtue and his responsibility to seek it, on his duty in the moral order, they failed too often to realize that the *political* condition of moral fulfillment is freedom from coercion.[22]

There is an important difference in emphasis on virtue between those "traditionalist" Conservatives who draw inspiration from Burke and those "libertarian" Conservatives who owe so much to nineteenth-century liberalism. While both groups agree that virtue and order are important to freedom, there is a differing emphasis on their exact importance and the degree to which the state may, in certain select cases, try to safeguard various moral standards. The "traditionalist" Conservatives do not argue that the state should try to control all aspects of human existence so as to compel the right kind of behavior. Like the "libertarian" Conservatives, the "traditionalist" Conservatives abhor the idea of a totalitarian state. But there are several social and political issues where differing emphasis on the idea of virtue makes itself manifest. The differences become most obvious in regard to issues concerning pornography, censorship, abortion, civil liberties, and the rights of homosexuals. In regard to these issues "libertarian"

Conservatives argue for greater freedom of expression, regardless of the values of the individual, so long as the individual does not engage in acts of coercion against his fellow-man. This response clearly reflects the impact of the classical liberal view of freedom upon contemporary Conservative thinking. But "traditionalist" Conservatives, drawing upon thinkers like Willmoore Kendall, Walter Berns, and Leo Strauss, argue that while freedom is important, consideration of virtue should lead the state, in certain cases, to try to uphold various moral standards.

Besides differing in the emphasis they give to the idea of virtue, the two groups of Conservatives also disagree on the emphasis that should be given to the idea of order. This difference plays a part in the debate between the two groups about matters relating to civil liberties. The "libertarian" Conservatives, being fearful of the state and wishing to maximize individual liberty, are strong supporters of civil liberties. The "traditionalist" Conservatives, giving more attention to the need for order in society, and believing in the need for a strong government to deal with the anarchic impulses within man, are more willing to limit civil liberties.

The differing importance that the two groups grant to notions of virtue, order, and the position of the state in relation to the freedom of the individual also leads them to disagree in regard to economic and political issues about the kind of responsibilities the state ought to exercise in regard to the lives of its citizens. This can be seen in their differences as to whether or not the state should act in a paternalistic fashion toward its citizens. This disagreement is one of the most crucial disputes dividing the two schools of Conservative thought. It reveals basic differences among Conservatives relating to a host of economic and political issues surrounding the modern welfare state. The "traditionalist" Conservatives, who can draw upon Conservatives such as Burke and Disraeli, adhere to an organic theory of society and sympathize with the idea of paternalistic government; they are able to support many aspects of the modern welfare state. These

Conservatives hold that it is the just responsibility of the government to care for its disadvantaged citizens in much the same way as parents ought to care for their children until they reach maturity.

The "libertarian" Conservatives, who are much more suspicious of the state than are the "traditionalist" Conservatives, believe that the idea of paternalistic government gives the state far too much power and responsibility over the lives of its citizens. They argue that individual freedom is somehow endangered by the welfare state and that steps ought to be taken to halt its growth. These Conservatives frequently argue that paternalistic government generates bureaucratic structures that are inimical to human freedom. For their views they rely heavily upon the works of contemporary classical liberal thinkers such as Friedrich Hayek and Milton Friedman. And they owe a considerable debt to nineteenth-century advocates of laissez-faire capitalism like William Graham Sumner, who not only defended a free-market economy but also lashed out at paternalistic government and lambasted "social reformers" in a way which is popular with many Conservatives even today.

It is interesting to note that English Conservatives, at least until Margaret Thatcher, have more often supported a "traditionalist" defense of paternalism, which is sympathetic to the modern welfare state, while American Conservatives have more often engaged in a "libertarian" critique of paternalism, which is hostile to the contemporary welfare state. Indeed, it would be difficult to understand the economic, budgetary, and regulatory policies of the Reagan administration without appreciating the intellectual debt that so many American Conservatives owe to laissez-faire liberals such as Sumner, Mises, Hayek, and Friedman.

Another disagreement that exists between the two groups of Conservatives because of their differing views on the exact relationship between virtue, freedom, and order is found in their differing attitudes toward the role of the state in a capitalist economy. Many "traditionalist" Conservatives are quite critical of unregulated capitalism. They view unregulated capitalism as an integral part of the materialism and hedonism they so dislike in the modern Western world; they spurn the civilization that has grown up around the capitalist order. They believe that unregulated capitalism has placed great burdens on the way of life they think necessary for the development of human freedom along virtuous lines. These Conservatives, such as Russell Kirk and Peter Viereck, whose primary concern is to emphasize the importance of culture and virtue, draw heavily from Conservative literary figures such as Coleridge in their attack on the bourgeois social and economic order. The most complete rejection of capitalism by this Conservative position is found in the works of Peter Viereck.

The "libertarian" Conservatives adopt a very different attitude toward capitalism. While often agreeing with the "traditionalist" Conservatives about the sad shape of modern culture, they argue that capitalism is not, by itself, to blame for this. Rather than evaluating capitalism in terms of whether or not it permits or hinders a high level of cultural development for the individual, the "libertarian" Conservative argues that the crucial question to ask is whether or not capitalism helps to create some of the conditions for human freedom by creating a great area in life that is outside the coercive powers of the state. These Conservatives argue that present alternatives to a capitalistic ordering of the economy are either economically unfeasible or would lead to the further accumulation of power by the state, which would be dangerous to individual freedom. Here again one sees the debt that these Conservatives owe to the classical liberal view of freedom. The "traditionalist" Conservatives are primarily interested in questions about culture and virtue when discussing capitalism; the "libertarian" Conservatives are more interested in political and economic questions that relate to the effects of capitalism on human freedom. Most contemporary American Conservatives are more influenced by the "libertarian" view of capitalism as essential to human freedom. Seldom will a

Conservative politician give a speech on economic policy in the United States without singing praises to the free-enterprise system as the source of America's economic achievements.

The crucial problem facing the internal coherence of the Conservative value system is whether or not the differences between the "traditionalist" and "libertarian" treatment of Conservative values are of an irreconcilable nature. The answer to this question depends on which level of thought, and to which issues, the question is posed. There does seem to be a philosophical level on which the two orientations can be reconciled. Even the "libertarian" position shares with the "traditionalist" position the belief in the great importance of all three values. Here one needs to distinguish the "libertarian" Conservatives from the "libertarians" of the Left (who are secular liberals) and the "libertarians" of the Right (who, following Ayn Rand, are staunch atheists). "Libertarian" Conservatives like Frank Meyer agree with the "traditionalist" Conservative position which holds that there is some kind of absolute moral ordering to the universe and that man's great duty in life is to cultivate virtue. The "libertarian" Conservative position still upholds some of the basic religious, moral, and metaphysical premises found in the "traditionalist" position.

But leaving this area of philosophical agreement, one immediately encounters levels of thought where the two positions cannot be reconciled. While the Conservative value system may have some coherence on an abstract philosophical level, it looses its coherence on matters of great importance relating to practical political and economic issues. It is difficult to see how the differences between the "traditionalist" and "libertarian" Conservatives in regard to such political and economic issues as the role of the state in a capitalist economy, the proper scope of civil liberties, and the just responsibilities of the state can be smoothed over. Certainly, the two groups of Conservatives are often allied in opposing many non-Conservative lines of thought. But the fact they often share common opponents does not cover up their own disagreements on which values should have priority in dealing with specific political questions. One might think here of how the Reagan administration receives conflicting advice from Conservatives on how to handle social issues such as abortion and pornography. This whole area of difficulty facing Conservative thought will play an important part in the discussion, in chapter six, of the relationship between theory and practice in Conservative thought. The reader who is particularly interested in the conflict between "libertarian" and "traditionalist" Conservatives would do well to read *The Conservative Intellectual Movement in America since 1945* by George H. Nash.

That Conservatives have so much trouble agreeing on how to rank and relate their basic values in dealing with so many political issues creates a considerable embarrassment for both Conservative moral theory and Conservative epistemology. Conservative moral theory claims that there is an objective moral ordering to the universe, and Conservative epistemology holds that it is possible to have knowledge about the ordering. But the knowledge about that ordering turns out to be only the most general and abstract kind of knowledge; just how the absolute moral ordering and the crucial values of virtue, freedom, and order are to be related to specific issues remains a matter of much debate among Conservatives. However, this is to be expected, given the pluralistic nature of the Conservative's value system. And while this generates conflict among Conservatives, it is no doubt preferable to the kind of dogmatism which would set up one value on a pedestal and sacrifice other important values to it.

5. Conservatism and the Foundations of Order: The Bases of the Good Society

The meaning and value of order is one of the most important themes found in Conservative thought. The Conservative view of order concerns the life of the individual as well as society at large. Moreover, Conservatives are interested in the *right* structuring of both. In explaining their view of the basis of such an ordering, one must explore seven basic themes of Conservative political theory. These basic themes are: (1) belief in tradition as the key to a stable society, (2) opposition to revolution as a means of restructuring society, (3) reliance on gradual reform as the way peacefully to change society while maintaining the basic features of the social and political order, (4) the role played by aristocratic elitism in answering the old political question of who should rule, (5) the Conservative's response to democratic politics and how to structure democracy so as to make possible a stable society, (6) concern with the decentralization of political structures and belief in community relationships as the basis of a well ordered and free society, (7) the perception that private property is an important institutional basis of the good society.

PART I: THE IMPORTANCE OF CULTURE
AND TRADITION

The Conservative discussion of the foundations of order for the life of the individual and society emphasizes the development of a nation's cultural life. Stressing the importance of culture reflects the predominance of "spiritual factors" in the Conservative's sociological analysis of society. The high place of these factors in such analysis is dictated by the underlying religious and moral premises of Conservative thought.

Conservatives argue that the development of a nation's cultural life is not something that can take place overnight. They believe that it is a task which must occupy the time and energy of several generations. Interest in the value of culture leads them to speak of the importance of traditions, of the passing on and development of culture over time. In this connection Burke delivers one of the most famous Conservative statements about the importance of tradition and the partnership between generations:

> Society is indeed a contract. Subordinate contracts for objects of mere occasional interests may be dissolved at pleasure—but the state ought not to be considered as nothing better than a partnership statement in trade of pepper and coffee, callico or tabacco, or some other such low concern, to be taken up for a little temporary interest, and to be dissolved by the fancy of the parties. It is to be looked on with other reverence; because it is not a partnership in things subservient only to the gross animal existence of a temporary and perishable nature. It is a partnership in all science; a partnership in all art; a partnership in every virtue, and in all perfection. As the ends of such a partnership cannot be obtained in many generations, it becomes a partnership not only between those who are living, but between those who are living, those who are dead, and those who are to be born.[1]

The continuity of that partnership between generations is

viewed by the Conservative as essential for both social stability and the right ordering of the life of the individual.

On a purely sociological level this view about the importance of a common culture and stable traditions can be applied to the analysis of the relative stability of many types of societies. It is on this level that Conservatism is often defined and discussed. Thus the view is held that Conservatism stands for the continuity of traditions, regardless of content, so long as some sort of status quo is maintained in the cultural life of the nation. While this view captures an important and popular meaning of what Conservatism stands for, it is also misleading because it omits normative considerations that play a major role in Conservative talk about the *right* kind of culture and traditions. Conservative complaints about the decline of Western civilization require the existence of normative standards by which different cultures and traditions may be evaluated. In this connection T. S. Eliot writes:

> The most important question that we can ask, is whether there is any permanent standard, by which we can compare one civilisation with another, and by which we can make some guess at the improvement or decline of our own. We have to admit, in comparing one civilisation with another, and in comparing the different stages of our own, that no one society and no one age of it realises all the values of civilisation. Not all of these values may be compatible with each other: what is at least as certain is that in realising some we lose the appreciation of others. Nevertheless, we can distinguish between higher and lower cultures; we can distinguish between advance and retrogression. We can assert with some confidence that our own period is one of decline; that the standards of culture are lower than they were fifty years ago; and that the evidences of this decline are visible in every department of human activity.[2]

Conservatives are not only interested in the stability of traditions, they are also interested in the moral worth of traditions.

Natural law becomes one standard by which traditions are evaluated.

The manner in which Conservatism both includes the sociological level of thinking, and transcends it, in order to deal with normative issues becomes clearer when one examines its view about which beliefs and practices are so important for healthy cultures and traditions. The idea that religious and moral beliefs serve as the basis of viable cultures finds expression in T. S. Eliot's assertion:

> The first important assertion is that no culture has appeared or developed except together with a religion: according to the point of view of the observer, the culture will appear to be the product of the religion, or the religion the product of the culture.[3]

Conservative statements about the importance of religious and moral beliefs can be approached on both the sociological and normative levels. On the first level there is concern with the general effects of such beliefs on the stability of society, while on the normative level most Western Conservatives believe that Christianity and the basic values expressed by theocentric humanism serve as the foundations for the proper kind of culture and traditions.

Stanley Parry provides a description of the function that Conservatives believe a healthy culture and set of traditions should serve:

> The essential thing is that civilization is a system based on the communication of inner perceptions of the truth about man. Thus a common tradition enables men who differ widely as to actual moral achievement to live in a life in common. The shared principles structure the community. The structuring is publicly organized, and normally is established by processes whose sanction lies in the fact that they do implement the view of the good held to be true by all. We can say, in brief, that a civilization exists in the first instance when a multitude of natures are open to

each other for communication on the level of moral perception. When natures are closed to each other, there is no civilization. It has fallen out of existence, even though the massive exoskeleton of buildings and technology still exist. A tradition exists as the ordering principle of a multitude precisely when it exists in the soul of each member and constitutes thereby the opening from each to every other soul. If there is no such opening, there is no tradition, even though the symbols of the tradition continue to exist and receive a formalized recognition.[4]

Conservatism holds that the right kind of tradition is one which permits the development of spiritual communication among individuals, that permits the opening of one soul to another. Good traditions encourage the flowering of theocentric humanism. They provide direction for the individual by helping to form his soul according to what Conservatives believe to be certain truths about God, man, and the universe; they promote peace within society by guiding the interaction among individuals according to a wide range of commonly accepted beliefs.

Conservatives hold that tradition provides a valuable framework for the functioning of human reason. They believe that for human reason to function properly it must operate in the context of a sound, healthy set of traditions. They argue that this is especially true for moral and political reasoning because well-accepted traditions provide enough common ground where different individuals may understand and communicate with each other in a sympathetic manner so that, despite their differences, the peace of society may be preserved.

Conservatives maintain that liberalism undermines the social order by turning loose critical reason upon tradition. In doing this liberalism erodes the social bonds and sentiments necessary for the responsible use of personal freedom. T. S. Eliot writes:

By destroying traditional social habits of the people, by

dissolving their natural collective consciousness into individual constituents, by licensing the opinions of the most foolish, by substituting instruction for education, by encouraging cleverness rather than wisdom, the upstart rather than the qualified, by fostering a notion of *getting on* to which the alternative is a hopeless apathy, Liberalism can prepare the way for that which is its own negation: the artificial, mechanised or brutalised control which is a desperate remedy for its chaos.[5]

Conservatives fear that the social problems that beset modern Western society cannot be easily resolved by reason because the necessary prerequisite for reason's successful operation—the existence of a viable tradition of common premises—has been damaged. Conservatives argue that with the decline of the Judeo-Christian tradition and the values of theocentric humanism, the common ground for genuine communication and peaceful persuasion among individuals is diluted, and modern society is forced to rely upon more coercive means of social control. This view only intensifies the pessimism that traditionalist Conservatives feel in regard to modern society, for they believe that modern Western society is cut off from the means to resolve its own crises. Stanley Parry argues in support of this position:

> The radical inability of reason to solve the problem of a crisis in civilization rests essentially on the fact that in all moral reason there is a necessary element of subjectivity. As a result of this element, the methods of persuasion, the only ones available to reason, collapse with the disappearance of the social pre-conditions necessary for the process of persuasion. Since the basic pre-condition is a commonly accepted moral order, it follows almost by definition that in a collapse of tradition, i.e., of a commonly accepted moral order, reason becomes helpless.[6]

It is important to keep in mind that Conservatives are interested in the right kind of traditions. While they are often defenders of the status quo, given the proper traditions, other times they are anything but friendly toward the status quo or a given culture. With Burke one is dealing with a form of Conservatism that, at least on the surface, could defend the cultural status quo and feel reasonably at home in a given tradition. He could write:

> Thanks to our sullen resistance to innovation, thanks to the cold sluggishness of our national character, we still bear the stamp of our forefathers. We have not (as I conceive) lost the generosity and dignity of thinking of the fourteenth century; nor as yet have we subtilized ourselves into savages. We are not the converts of Rousseau; we are not the disciples of Voltaire; Helvetius has made no progress amongst us. Atheists are not our preachers, madmen are not our lawgivers.[7]

Burke is able to express an attitude toward the traditions of his own nation that represents "natural Conservatism."

But contemporary Conservatives must face the culture and traditions of their society in a different way, "natural Conservatism" being impossible given the content of contemporary culture. Frank Meyer is forced to write:

> Like Socrates, Plato, and Aristotle, confronting the chaos in the body politic and in the minds of men created by the overweening pride of the Athenian *demos*, we do not live in the happy age of a natural conservatism. We cannot simply revere; we cannot uncritically follow tradition, for the tradition presented to us is rapidly becoming —thanks to the prevailing intellectual climate, thanks to the schools, thanks to the outpourings of all the agencies that mold opinion and belief—the tradition of a positivism scornful of truth and virtue, the tradition of the collective, the tradition of the untrammeled state.[8]

This leads to a situation in which some Conservatives speak against the status quo and for overthrowing it. Thus, Willmoore Kendall and George Carey write:

Conservative resistance may in certain circumstances (for example, in a society or organization or activity that at an earlier moment has passed under more or less complete control by progressive changers and innovators), express itself in the desire to overthrow the *status quo* and the tradition or orthodoxy to which it points as its justification. The conservative may, that is to say, regard himself as the defender of a tradition or orthodoxy which, though it has been reduced to a mere remnant, he continues to insist upon as *the* tradition or *the* orthodoxy appropriate to that organization or activity.[9]

On the political and economic levels this is the position in which the Reagan administration finds itself as it challenges many aspects of the liberalism of the New Deal and the Great Society. The Reagan administration is Conservative, yet it also wants to alter the status quo. It attacks an existing orthodoxy in the name of older American traditions. And at least part of the irony of what the Reagan administration is trying to do is that its critique of contemporary liberalism owes so much to nineteenth-century laissez-faire liberalism.

Modern Conservatives thus find themselves in a curious position when speaking of tradition. They are forced to pick and choose when they speak of the importance of certain traditions, for often they must attack what is now traditional in the name of older traditions. This complicates the nature of their relationship to their own society and creates difficulties for many aspects of their thought.

These difficulties can be seen in how contrary styles of thinking come to characterize the thought of different Conservatives. As Frank Meyer points out:

The tendency to establish false antitheses obstructing fruitful confrontation arises in part from an inherent dilemma of conservatism in a revolutionary era, such as ours. There is a real contradiction between the deep piety of the conservative spirit towards tradition, prescription, the preservation of the fiber of society (what has been called

"natural conservatism") and the more reasoned, consciously principled, militant conservatism which becomes
necessary when the fibers of society have been rudely torn
apart, when deleterious revolutionary principles ride high,
and restoration, not preservation, is the order of the day.[10]

The result of all this is that the Conservative's actual relation
to tradition in the last part of the twentieth century has become more complex and less intelligible than, say, the relationship Burke had with the traditions of his own time. The
ties between Conservatism and traditionalism become weaker
as modernity advances.

The dilemma that Conservatism faces in regard to modern
society also reflects itself in the conflict between the traditionalist and natural-law elements of Conservative thought.
One critic of Conservative thought, Morton Auerbach,
makes a comment about the problems facing the ancient
Stoics which may also be used to help explain some of the
conflicts found in modern Conservative thinking. Auerbach
writes:

> Stoicism was the adjustment of Conservatism to these
> new historical conditions. The Early Stoics, who lived at
> the end of the fourth and beginning of the third centuries
> B.C., made the initial transition by emphasizing that the
> individual, who was now socially isolated, must look to the
> world society, the "brotherhood of man," for his "commu-
> nity." Moreover, since morality could no longer depend
> upon clear social norms, the individual must seek the uni-
> versal elements of morality—the "natural law"—within
> his own conscience and reason.[11]

With the decline of the kinds of traditions that Conservatism
supports, and with the decline of rural and hierarchial community relationships in the modern world, many Conservatives, like the ancient Stoics before them, have turned to a
natural-law mode of thinking about morality and politics.
While Burke certainly supported the idea of natural law,

he never really went to much trouble to develop his conception of it. His thinking remained, for the most part, within the context of the traditionalist mode of thought. Supporters of natural-law thinking have generally been critical of Burke for not developing in greater detail his conception of natural law. But within the context of Conservative thought it was not really necessary that Burke do such a thing in order to defend his values. He could still draw, in a very direct manner, upon certain traditions which are not easily accessible to modern Conservatives. In the natural Conservatism of Burke one encounters a traditionalist mode of thinking that is nontheoretical, highly empirical and pragmatic, confortably adjusted to its social environment. This kind of thinking shys away from the abstract and always emphasizes the concrete details of society.

But in twentieth-century Conservative thought one encounters a style of thinking that is more theoretical and abstract. Many Conservatives turn to Voegelin and Strauss for philosophical guidance and introduce a natural-law and rationalistic flavoring to their thinking. The decline of supporting traditions and the decay of organic community relationships force Conservative thought, despite its original intentions, to become more theoretical and abstract. At the same time this works against the internal unity of Conservative thought. While many Conservatives turn to more theoretical, rationalistic, and natural-law modes of thought, others still try to preserve traditionalist modes of thinking, despite the awkwardness that this involves.

Contemporary Conservatism is caught in a difficult position in regard to modernity. Emphasis on the proper kinds of traditions is a crucial part of the Conservative view of what constitutes the foundations of a healthy and stable social order. But Conservatism faces great problems explaining how to restore a set of traditions it believes to have been seriously damaged. Some Conservatives even argue that it is impossible to restore artificially a culture and set of traditions once they have been lost or reduced to a mere remnant; they can see no political solution to the problem. As T. S. Eliot points out:

> The question asked by this essay is whether there are any permanent conditions, in absence of which no higher culture can be expected. If we succeed even partially in answering this question, we must put ourselves on guard against this delusion of trying to bring about these conditions *for the sake* of the improvement of our culture. For if any definite conclusions emerge from this study, one of them is surely this, that culture is the one thing that we cannot deliberately aim at. It is the product of a variety of more or less harmonious activities, each pursued for its own sake: the artist must concentrate upon his canvas, the poet upon his typewriter, the civil servant upon the just settlement of particular problems as they present themselves upon his desk, each according to the situation in which he finds himself. Even if these conditions with which I am concerned, seem to the reader to represent desirable social aims, he must not leap to the conclusion that these aims can be fulfilled solely by deliberate organization.[12]

This point made by T. S. Eliot only adds to the pessimism that many traditionalist Conservatives feel in regard to modern society.

The Reagan administration may find it much easier to change economic, budgetary, and regulatory policies than to repair the moral and cultural damage done to American society in the last two decades. Our knowledge of how to undo the harm inflicted upon the American family, religion, education, and community life trails our knowledge of how to achieve economic growth and stability (not that our knowledge in this area is all that substantial). How to win Congressional votes on budget and tax cuts may be relatively simple when compared to discovering what to do about pornography, abortion, the trashy character of commercial television and popular music, declining academic achievement in our schools, the high divorce rate, and declining community bonds. A more efficient federal government and a healthier economy by no means offer a solution to the moral and cultural illnesses afflicting American society.

There may be from time to time discussion of the need for a "religious revival" or "moral reawakening," and at present some Americans have hope for the "Moral Majority." But given the sharp Conservative critique of contemporary society, it is difficult to see how such efforts could produce any kind of genuine spiritual renaissance.

There are other problems facing the Conservative view of culture and tradition. A major problem arises because of the nonpolitical character of the Conservative view of culture. The nonpolitical character of most of the moral traditions Conservatism holds to be so important to a sound culture can be seen by examining C. S. Lewis' collection of moral precepts found in the appendix of his *The Abolition of Man*. His collection of traditional moral principles is drawn from the great religions of world history and contains only a few political ideas. Even a highly political Conservative, such as Quintin Hogg, is forced to admit to the nonpolitical flavoring that Conservative thought has because of its stress on culture:

> For Conservatives do not believe that political struggle is the most important thing in life. In this they differ from Communists, Socialists, Nazis, Fascists, Social Creditors, and most members of the British Labour Party. The simplest among them prefer fox-hunting—the wisest religion. To the great majority of Conservatives, religion, art, study, family, friends, music, fun, duty, all the joys and riches of existence of which the poor no less than the rich are the indefeasible freeholders, all these are higher in the scale than their handmaiden, the political struggle.[13]

The trouble that this creates for Conservative thought is that

it is not always easy to translate its cultural values into political positions. It is difficult to see just how the nonpolitical
values of the Conservative are related to his political theory.
Certainly one can use these values for the negative function
of ruling out the most extreme and inhuman political theories
and of attacking states which violate the most cherished
values. However, it is more difficult to see just which positive
political actions the state ought to take in order to preserve
these nonpolitical values.

An even greater problem facing the Conservative involves
the question of what attitude to adopt toward cultures and
traditions which exist outside the framework of Western
civilization. Here the Conservative must choose between devotion to stability and devotion to truth. Concern for order
in general, along with the traditionalist, relativist, and sociological elements of the Conservative's thinking, lead him
to argue that non-Western societies should strive to preserve
their own cultures and traditions. The traditionalist mode of
Conservative thinking sympathizes with non-Western traditions. One can recall here Burke's attack on the British assault on native culture and traditions in India, or think of
Conservative criticisms of the Maoist assault on the Confu-
cian traditions in China.

However, there are also natural-law, absolutist, and normative elements to the Conservative's thinking which lead
him to be concerned with truth and the right kind of culture
and traditions. This aspect of Conservative thought leads one
to argue that many non-Western societies should alter their
systems so as to accommodate certain Western religious,
moral, and political beliefs. But on a sociological level Conservative thought suggests that such an undertaking might
only produce chaos in non-Western societies.

Thus, the Conservative is in a taxing position, for it is difficult to tell Western man how to repair damaged traditions,
and it is even harder to decide what to say to non-Western
man.

PART II: THE CONSERVATIVE OPPOSITION
TO REVOLUTION

The Conservative view of the sources of order in society can be further illuminated by examining what it takes to be the most extreme form of a disordered society. This leads immediately to consideration of the Conservative view of revolution. Conservatism holds that a society falling victim to revolution is the classic case of a disordered society and that it is in such a society where one can find prime examples of complete disorientation in the life of the individual. A society undergoing revolution stands in the sharpest contrast to the kind of society the Conservative views as rightly ordered. The members of a rightly ordered society share common traditions and values which unite them in peaceful association. However, in a society undergoing a revolution the population loses the common traditions that serve as a basis for moral and political unity.

One of the central themes of Conservative thought is its general opposition to revolution as a strategy for improving the condition of mankind and its rejection of the idea that out of revolution can grow the seeds of a just restructuring of society. One of the reasons why Conservatives feel so alienated in the modern world lies in their general opposition to the revolutions that have occurred in the last three centuries.

The Conservative presumption against revolution as a strategy for improving the lot of mankind holds that it is a very dubious undertaking which gambles the lives of a whole generation on a vision of happiness for future generations. Conservatives agree with Burke when he writes:

> The burden of proof lies heavily on those who tear to pieces the whole frame and contexture of their country, that they could find no other way of settling a government fit to obtain its rational ends, except that which they have pursued by means unfavorable to all the present happiness of millions of people, and to the utter ruin of several hun-

dreds of thousands. In their political arrangements, men
have no right to put the well-being of the present generation wholly out of the question. Perhaps the only moral
trust with any certainty in our hands, is the care of our own
time. With regard to futurity, we are to treat it like a ward.
We are not so to attempt an improvement of his fortune, as
to put the capital of his estate to any hazard.[14]

This distrust of revolution as a strategy for improving the lot
of mankind owes much to what some authors call the "Conservative temperament." For the Conservative the risk and
uncertainties that a revolutionary strategy involves make the
costs to be paid far too great.

What troubles the Conservative is what he considers to be
the mental attitude of the revolutionary. As pointed out in
chapter two, Conservatism holds that pride is man's greatest
sin. Perhaps the most sophisticated analysis of pride (as defined by Conservatism) can be found in Eric Voegelin's study
of the psychological attributes of gnosticism. In Voegelin's
analysis of the gnostic mentality, pride takes form in the
gnostic's desire to place himself in God's position. While Conservatives hold that all men are subject, at times, to the sin of
pride, they argue that in the case of the revolutionary, pride
appears in its most unchecked, arrogant, ungodly, and dangerous form. For the Conservative the pride of the revolutionary lies in the self-confidence of his vision of ideal justice
(what Voegelin terms the gnostic dream world) which he
seeks to impose upon the world and in the proud disdain and
contempt with which the revolutionary views all associated
with the system he desires to overthrow. In the Conservative's
eyes the revolutionary seeks to become and play God.

Conservatives argue that revolutionary thinking leads to
a situation in which men become so obsessed with a vision of
ideal justice, and so filled with hatred for the world around
them that, in Burke's words, "By hating vices too much, they
come to love men too little."[15] In the Conservative's eyes this
leads the revolutionary to sacrifice the lives of thousands,

sometimes millions, of people in an attempt to get rid of the vices of a social system. In the name of humanity, in the name of the highest ideals, the lives of people are sacrificed in order to "liberate them." According to the Conservative this leads to a distortion in the soul of the revolutionary, in which the revolutionary's moral judgment becomes warped by his hatred for the existing system. Burke writes:

> This sort of people are so taken up with their theories about the rights of man, that they have totally forgotten his nature. Without opening one new avenue to the understanding, they have succeeded in stopping up those that lead to the heart. They have perverted in themselves, and in those that attend to them, all the well-placed sympathies of the human breast.[16]

The horrors created by revolutionaries reconstructing society in the name of some vision of a purified, just social order can be seen in the second half of the 1970s by looking at events in Cambodia. There the Pol Pot regime managed, before the final invasion by the Vietnamese, to slaughter over a million of its own people in the name of liberating society from the corruptions of the past. All this was done in the name of revolution. Throughout the twentieth century revolutionaries in Russia, China, Cambodia, and a host of less visible situations have occasioned mass arrests, executions, concentration camps, and starvation alongside the most glowing rhetoric about improving the lot of the ordinary man. Revolutionaries in this century have left no evil untried in pursuing their various utopias.

Conservatives not only fear the effects of revolution in terms of lives lost, but they also fear the impact of revolution on peoples' moral and political judgments. Revolution in a society, according to the Conservative, creates a situation in which individuals are forced to choose between moral and political extremes. This means that prudence can no longer function. Conservatives hold that prudence should guide the individual in thinking about moral and political questions.

But the climate of extremes that a revolution produces destroys the climate of moderation necessary for the operation of prudence. The most clasic Conservative description of what revolution does to a society and to the moral judgments of individuals can be found in Thucydides' description of what revolution meant to the Greek city states in the Peloponnesian War:

> The sufferings which revolution entailed on the cities were many and terrible, such as have occurred and always will occur, as long as the nature of mankind remains the same; though in a severer or milder form, and varying in their particular cases. In peace and prosperity states and individuals have better sentiments, because they do not find themselves suddenly confronted with imperious necessities; but war takes away the easy supply of daily wants, and proves a rough master, that brings most men's characters to a level with their fortunes. Revolution thus ran its course from city to city, and the places which it arrived at last, from having heard what had been done before, carried to a still greater excess the refinement of their inventions, as manifested in the cunning of their enterprises and the atrocity of their reprisals. Words had to change their ordinary meaning and to take that to which was now given them. Reckless audacity came to be considered the courage of a loyal ally; prudent hesitation, specious cowardice; moderation was held to be a cloak for unmanliness; ability to see all sides of a question ineptness to act on any. Frantic violence became the attribute of manliness; cautious plotting a justifiable means of self defense. The advocate of extreme measures was always trustworthy; his opponent a man to be suspected.[17]

Conservatives fear that by warping the moral judgments of individuals revolution helps to destroy the possibility of a life of virtue for the individual.

What is interesting to note, and often escapes the attention of many Conservatives, is that the moral disorder found within a society undergoing a revolution affects the counter-revolutionary forces as well as the revolutionary forces. Thucydides' statement makes no distinction between the extremism and moral disorder characterizing the judgment of one side as opposed to the other side. Perhaps the real tragedy, from the standpoint of the Conservative, to be found in this characterization of the moral disorder present in a society undergoing revolution, is that the disorder affects even those who struggle against the revolutionary forces . . . even the counterrevolutionary may fall victim to the disorder. One need only think of what happened to French thinkers like Joseph de Maistre in order to understand how reactionary thought is developed in response to the chaos created by revolution.

A main objection against the general Conservative rejection of revolution as a strategy for improving the condition of mankind is made along the following lines: Conservatives give all their attention to the costs of revolution, to the violence, cruelty, and moral disorder that revolution involves. But they fail to see the same kind of costs that are involved in maintaining the kinds of systems which have been the objects of revolution. They fail to consider the possibility that the long-run costs of preserving certain social systems may be much greater than the costs of a revolution. The gains of a successful revolution, in doing away with an oppressive social order, may outweigh the costs of revolution.

While this line of criticism may hold true of some Conservatives, it does not hold true of all of them. One need only read Conservative anti-Communist tracts directed against the Russian and Chinese systems in order to see just how critical Conservatives can be in regard to the costs of continuing certain social systems. The works of Aleksander Solzhenitsyn are most appropriate in this connection. Totalitarian regimes, where the evil the government perpetrates upon society is so great and the chances for reform so small, provide a situation where many Conservatives would risk revolution.

One can also see Conservatives paying a great deal of attention to the costs of preserving their own social system when one examines their various critiques of Western society. Here one might consider what critics of abortion have to say about the terrible price society pays for accepting the norms of secular liberalism. Conservatives, because they do recognize man's moral shortcomings, are not blind to the costs of preserving a given status quo.

However, while Conservatives see the costs of preserving various social systems, they generally oppose revolution as a means of dealing with the problem. This is not because they fail to understand the case that might be made for revolution, particularly in totalitarian nations. Conservatives may even accept the general argument that if one could be sure that a significantly more just social system would emerge from a revolution against a despicable social system, then a revolution might be justified. Burke writes:

> Without attempting therefore to define, what never can be defined, the case of a revolution in government, this, I think, may be safely affirmed, that a sore and pressing evil is to be removed, and that a good, great in its amount, and unequivocal in its nature, must be probable almost to certainty, before the inestimable price of our own morals, and the well-being of a number of our fellow-citizens, is paid for a revolution.[18]

However, Conservatives hold that revolution introduces such uncertainties and unpredictability into the equation that there is usually little assurance a significantly better system will emerge from the revolution. Here one can see the importance of what some authors term the "Conservative temperament," which includes a great distaste for risk-taking.

Conservatives argue that revolution helps create a climate within society that usually makes the emergence of a superior social system doubtful. Since the Conservative holds that a society undergoing a revolution is characterized by a form of moral disorder which warps the judgment of the members of society, he fears the only way that order of any kind can be restored to such a society is by force. Because the society has lost its common moral traditions which make possible peaceful association between citizens, and because the revolution forces both supporters and opponents into extreme situations which warp their moral judgments, the Conservative argues that the winning side will probably be compelled to use force and terror. The use of force and terror, by either the victorious revolutionary or counterrevolutionary factions, is likely to generate institutional mechanisms of oppression which will perpetuate themselves in the newly created social order, making doubtful the emergence of a just regime. This view is supported by the results of so many twentieth-century revolutions in which totalitarian political parties took the lead in overthrowing unjust authoritarian regimes, creating even more oppression.

Yet another criticism of the Conservative's view of revolution calls into question his concern with the revolutionary mentality. This line of criticism holds that the Conservative is so preoccupied with the revolutionary mentality that he forgets the "real" causes of revolution which are supposed to give rise to the revolutionary mentality in the first place. The radical holds that the Conservative is so concerned with the "spiritual factors" (the attitudes and beliefs of the revolutionary) that he overlooks the political, economic, and social factors which lead to the revolutionary situation. The radical holds that a revolutionary group is usually forced into doing what it does by the oppressive nature of the existing system. In the analysis of revolution the Conservative centers his attention on what he calls the revolutionary mentality, whereas the radicals concentrate on the kind of factors they believe give birth to that mentality. The Conservative approach leads to a condemnation of the revolutionary, while the radical approach to the subject leads to some kind of sociological explanation and justification of the revolutionary. But since not all unjust societies produce revolution, and many are successfully reformed, the Conservative argues that revolutionaries make the revolution and bear responsibility for the often disastrous results.

Since the Conservative usually rules out revolution as a strategy for improving the lot of mankind, the question that can then be asked concerns just what alternative he gives to those individuals who believe they live in a system standing in great need of change. This leads immediately to the Conservative view of reformism. As will be shown, Conservatives believe that the capacity of a society to engage in successful reforms constitutes an important source of order and stability for that society.

PART III: THE CONSERVATIVE VIEW OF REFORM

Contrary to the popular image held of Conservatives, they do recognize that existing societies are full of defects and often stand in need of reform. The idea of reform plays an important role in their political and social thought. It also helps to bring into focus certain aspects of their opposition to revolution.

One of the chief reasons that Conservatives give for supporting reform strategies for improving the lot of mankind is that such strategies may help to prevent revolution. They argue that the ability of a state to engage in successful reforms is a key to its survival. Burke writes:

> A state without the means of some change is without the means of its conservation. Without such means it might ever risque the loss of that part of the constitution which it wished the most religiously to preserve.[19]

The heart of this view of reform is the belief that the chief task of reform is to preserve the basic features of society while trying to deal with various social problems on a piecemeal, one at a time, nonsystematic basis. Klaus Epstein captures the spirit of Conservative reformism when he writes:

The Reform Conservative will always seek to maximize continuity; when encountering a defective institution, he will try reform before consenting to its abolition; he will, if possible, pour new wine into old bottles rather than create completely new institutions to cope with new needs. His action will always aim at rearranging the elements of the existing structure of society instead of aiming at a total reconstruction *de novo*; his reform work will be done in sorrow rather than in anger, in a spirit of reluctant bowing to necessity rather than joyful triumph. He will view with reverence what was valuable in the past even though it must be eliminated for the sake of the future; and he will seek to maintain an over-all pattern of society where the old will always overbalance the new.[20]

The incrementalism of the Conservative reform strategy, in contrast to the wholesale nature of radical reformism, can be seen in R. J. White's statement:

To discover the order which inheres in things rather than to impose an order upon them; to strengthen and perpetuate that order rather than to dispose things anew according to some formula which may be nothing more than a fashion; to legislate along the grain of human nature rather than against it; to pursue limited objectives with a watchful eye; to amend here, to prune there; in short, to preserve the method of nature in the conduct of the state— because nature, as Burke observed, is wisdom without reflection and above it: this is Conservatism. Its method is Aristotelian, its temper sceptical.[21]

Conservative reformism stays clear of the kind of radical reformism which attempts a total reconstruction of society. Radical reformism aims at fundamental change in social structure. The Conservative reformer is much more cautious about what can really be changed and is more skeptical about the knowledge reformers claim to have as they go about trying to alter society.

The greatest problem facing such reformism concerns its applicability to different societies and whether it is always an adequate means of defending Conservative values or of creating a situation more favorable to such values. Holding that reform is the great alternative to revolution as a strategy for improving the lot of mankind, Conservative reformism rests upon an important premise expressed by Burke:

> But in this, as in most questions of state, there is a middle. There is something else than the mere alternative of absolute destruction, or unreformed existence.[22]

Burke's assumption, that there is usually a viable alternative to unreformed existence and revolution, is essential for Conservative reformism. The difficulty is that in many societies there are good reasons to doubt the truth of Burke's assumption. In many societies the forces opposed to needed reforms have been so powerful that there has been little chance of the reforms ever being adopted in what would be regarded as a reasonable period of time by those being oppressed. Conservative reformism has little applicability to such societies.

There is the problem of what can the Conservative say on the subject of reform and revolution in a regime he regards as totally corrupt and oppressive but incapable of any kind of reasonable reforms. What does the Conservative have to say to those who live under regimes which are oppressive by his own standards and are incapable of adopting what he would view as needed reforms? What can the American Conservative say to those people of the Soviet Union and China opposed to Communism? Conservatives, if always rejecting revolution, and given the limited applicability of their reform strategy, would have little to say to those millions of people in the world they view as most oppressed. Here is where opposition to revolution cannot be absolute, despite the terrible risks and doubtful outcome of such an undertaking. Here is where many Conservatives would justify revolution. But such a justification would not be made out of zeal or naive assumptions about the outcome. It would be made out of desperation.

The key to the Conservative reform strategy lies in the capacity of a society to engage in the kinds of reforms that both meet the needs of the oppressed and preserve the basic features of that social order. This in turn requires two things. First, the historical conditions within that society must be such that the above requirements are not contradictory. Second, those who hold power in that society must have both the will and the intelligence to undertake the necessary reforms. This leads immediately to consideration of the Conservative view of leadership within society. The Conservative's theory of leadership is one of the basic themes of his political thought; he believes that the successful preservation of social order depends upon strong and wise leadership on the part of the governing elite.

PART IV: ARISTOCRATIC ELITISM

Conservatism has, historically, had a strong elitist orientation in its view of who should lead in society and how to best organize society. In answer to the question of where to look for those individuals who are exceptionally qualified to lead in a society, eighteenth- and early nineteenth-century Conservatism generally pointed to the aristocracy. Conservatives argued that the position, qualifications, and virtues of the aristocracy, because of its special way of life and training, made it especially fit to direct the political life and destiny of the nation. Even in the twentieth century one may find some Conservatives arguing for the need of societal leadership under a virtuous aristocracy. T. S. Eliot writes:

> In a healthily *stratified* society, public affairs would be a responsibility not equally borne; a greater responsibility would be inherited by those who inherited special advantages, and in whom self-interest, and interest for the sake of their families ("a stake in the country") should cohere with public spirit. The governing elite, of the nation as a

whole, would consist of those whose responsibility was inherited with their affluence and position, and whose forces were constantly increased, and often led by rising individuals of exceptional talents.[23]

There are several reasons why the Conservative would be attracted to the idea of political leadership by a landed aristocracy. The tradition-bound way of life of such an aristocracy would make it look favorably upon traditions in general, and hopefully the aristocracy would try to preserve the kinds of traditions which the Conservative views as essential to the right ordering of society. The interests of such an aristocracy would make it a bulwark against revolution. An enlightened aristocracy, wishing to avoid revolution, would try to prevent a great number of people from being forced into a predicament of having to choose between unreformed existence and the absolute destruction of society. The Conservative would also want the reform process to be guided by such an aristocracy so that the reforms would not be allowed to endanger the basic structure of society.

The problem facing this veneration for aristocratic elitism has been that so many aristocracies have not lived up to the attributes the Conservative assigns to the good aristocracy. Many aristocracies have not been enlightened enough to carry out what the Conservative would regard as prudent reforms. Still other aristocracies have found themselves in a historical context in which the reforms they might have been willing to make could never satisfy the demands of the revolutionary forces.

One might think here of the incompetence of the French aristocracy prior to the Revolution. Many Conservatives have contrasted the disastrous French example with the English aristocracy, using the two as ideal types of what elites should and should not do, of the healthy and degenerate forms of aristocracy. The French aristocracy failed to live up to the kinds of duties and responsibilities to be expected from a good aristocracy. It lived for its fuedal rights and forgot its duties to provide leadership for society. The superiority of the English aristocracy lay in its ability to maintain its will to govern and lead society, in its ability to adapt to changing economic and political circumstances, and in its willingness to live up to the duties and responsibilities the Conservative believes a governing elite should live by. But gradually, throughout the nineteenth and twentieth centuries, despite the adaptability of the English aristocracy, it too began to lose its power and place in society. The aristocratic elite has gradually had to yield power to other elites. The greatest problem facing the Conservative support for aristocratic elitism was that the landed aristocracy was disappearing. What many Conservatives had to say about the aristocracy simply did not correspond with reality.

In America the Conservative veneration for aristocratic elitism has always been in a rather awkward position. First of all, American Conservatism lacked the feudal background which helped to form European Conservatism. Second, the aristocracy praised by many "traditionalist" Conservatives— the aristocracy represented by Washington, Jefferson, and the antebellum South—was marred by the institution of slavery (which is impossible to reconcile with Conservatism's theocentric humanism). Twentieth-century agrarian Conservatives in the United States have had to romanticize the Southern aristocracy and either try to apologize for or ignore the slavery question. Third, the industrialization of the United States, with the domination of American society by very different kinds of elites, has made Conservative talk about aristocratic elitism rather quaint. While the political and intellectual achievements of the Southern aristocracy were considerable, particularly in the case of Virginia's contribution to the founding of the American Republic, such an aristocracy no longer exists.

Twentieth-century Conservatism is in a difficult position regarding traditional support for aristocratic elitism. The class basis of the traditional Conservative view of who is to lead society has evaporated. Conservatives can no longer

point to a specific class or group possessing a special claim
to leadership. However, even though the Conservative cannot today rely upon an aristocratic ruling class, he still argues
that at least the aristocratic spirit must be preserved as a
necessary source of order for society. In the context of a modern, advanced industrial society the Conservative veneration
of aristocratic elitism, unable to rely upon a certain class,
must hope to find individuals who are still motivated by aristocratic values. Conservatives argue that the stability and
proper ordering of modern society depends upon finding such
individuals. Unable to find a specific social class to exercise
leadership in society, the Conservative must support the idea
of a meritocracy, where position and leadership are based
upon individual ability and merit. This is a major change for
Conservative political thought. Such a decision, to support
individual excellence over a superior social class, is a basic
concession to the principles of nineteenth-century liberalism.
It is both a social and political concession which marks a
crucial difference between contemporary Conservatism and
the aristocratic Conservatism of the late eighteenth and early
nineteenth centuries. It is also a door through which many
other aspects of liberal thought have passed into the framework of Conservatism.

The Conservative's analysis of the sources of order and disorder in society, unable to rely upon an aristocratic elite as a
source of stability, faces the task of coming to grips with the
question of order in the context of modern democratic political systems. This leads immediately to consideration of what
Conservatism has to say about modern democracy.

PART V: THE CONSERVATIVE RESPONSE TO
DEMOCRATIC POLITICS

One of the chief problems of modern Conservative thought
has been to show the means of preserving some of its most
important values in the context of modern democratic poli-

tics. In this discussion Conservatives are not always operating in what they would regard as a favorable environment. There are aspects of this environment that they have little control over and can do little about. They are bound to view certain aspects of modern society as inherently disordered. Yet, they still face the task of showing how to preserve or help to create as much order as possible under given circumstances.

While Conservative supporters of aristocratic elitism were at first critical of the emergence of democracy in modern times, gradually Anglo-American Conservatives came to be more receptive to democratic politics. This was especially true in America, where much of Conservative political thinking rests upon veneration of a group of Founding Fathers who helped to create a more democratic political system.

Conservatives have discovered that a democratic political system can, under the right circumstances, enhance social stability by providing for peaceful means of social and political change. Democratic majorities can be persuaded to be defenders of private property and supporters of limited government based on the rule of law and constitutionalism. By requiring those who would govern to seek popular support in free and competitive elections, democracy compels those who would hold office to pay attention to the interests of those who are governed.

This is not to suggest that Conservatives are naive in their acceptance of democracy. They are quite concerned over the quality of leaders chosen under democratic regimes. They also worry about the damage often done to society by democratic factionalism. They agree with James Madison's position in *Federalist Paper* No. 10: factions are the greatest problem facing popular government. Crucial to understanding the acceptance that Conservatives give to democratic politics is the qualified nature of their support. Like Madison, Conservatives are especially concerned with how to prevent irrational and populistic majorities from getting out of hand. They fear that an unrestrained democratic regime can be as dangerous as any other political regime; popular majorities can be as abusive of individual rights as unpopular dictators. The Conservative agrees with John Adams' argument that democracy, like any other form of government, must be limited:

> The fundamental article of my political creed is, that despotism, or unlimited sovereignty, or absolute power, is the same in a majority of a popular assembly, an aristocratical council, an oligarchical junto, and a single emperor. Equally arbitrary, cruel, bloody, and in every respect diabolical.[24]

The checks that Conservatives wish placed on democracy range from cultural to institutional restraints.

The first kind of check that the Conservatives believe should be placed on democracy is in the area of cultural restraints. They argue that a stable democratic regime requires a healthy society founded upon religious and moral traditions which limit the greed and irrationality of people. They believe that the spiritual life of the nation should be guided by an aristocratic love of human freedom and an aristocratic code of civic duties and responsibilities.

What is involved here is making democratic majorities, as well as the leaders they elect, respectful of the rights and interests of others in the society. This requires the maintenance of a political culture that downplays individual aggrandizement and emphasizes a code of conduct which says that leaders and popular majorities ought not to do certain things in pursuing their goals. These are internal checks upon democracy; they require the development of conscience and respect for the life positions of other citizens.

Such views lead traditionalist Conservatives to be concerned over the future course of contemporary, wealthy, secular democracies. They wonder how affluent, secular democracies can survive as morally healthy and well-ordered societies. First, with the decline of authority, religion, and moral traditions, the internal checks on the behavior of leaders and popular majorities are weakened. Second, there is a suspicion that a too soft and comfortable life style might sap the aristocratic spirit, with its special love for human freedom and corresponding acceptance of duties and responsibilities. Many Conservatives wonder about the ability of contemporary Western societies to maintain an orderly and virtuous form of freedom. And they have doubts about whether the populations and leaders of the West have retained sufficient vision and self-discipline to meet the Soviet challenge.

It is well worth noting that the greatest testament to the strength of the human spirit and the love of freedom in the second half of the twentieth century is to be found in the person and works of Aleksander Solzhenitsyn, an individual whose world view is at complete odds with the vision that the secular, liberal society of the West has of itself. Indeed, his critique of Western society is much like the attack of the ancient Hebrew prophets upon their own corrupt societies. His critique of the West suggests that its leaders and people suffer from moral decay at home and lack of vision in dealing with enemies abroad.

The Conservative believes that the moral damage inflicted upon Western culture in the past two decades has made the job of governing these democracies much more difficult. Materialistic pursuit of self-interests has made Western leaders and populations less responsible to their duties, more subject to factionalism, and more dangerous to themselves and others.

A primary concern in qualifying democratic politics relates to the desire to check the powers of majorities. Burke writes:

> If I recollect rightly, Aristotle observes that a democracy has many striking points of resemblance with a tyranny. Of this I am certain, that in a democracy, the majority of the citizens is capable of exercising the most cruel oppressions upon the minority, whenever strong divisions

prevail in that kind of polity, as they often must; and that oppression of the majority will extend to far greater numbers, and will be carried on with much greater fury, than can almost ever be apprehended from the dominion of a single sceptre.[25]

Conservatives are thus concerned with developing institutional checks on the powers of majorities. These institutional checks are meant to complement the cultural checks which the Conservative hopes will restrain the people and their leaders.

American Conservatism gives considerable attention to constitutional theories which limit and divide the power of majorities, divide the levels and powers of government, and stagger elections in such a way as to thwart populistic notions of political representation. Conservatives have drawn heavily from the *Federalist Papers* in support of their arguments for a limited, constitutional form of democracy. Conservatives like Willmoore Kendall, in opposing populistic forms of democracy, have gone to great lengths to develop a notion of cultivating "the deliberate will" of the people as opposed to their immediate will (which the Conservative fears may be reckless). What this means is that the Conservative believes a democratic political system should have strong constitutional and institutional checks on the powers of temporary majorities, so that changes in the system require majorities of a long-standing nature. Conservatives hope that such constitutional structuring of the system, and making the amending of the system a slow process, will help prevent the powers of temporary majorities (and the reform movements they generate) from getting out of hand and doing damage to the basic features of the system. Constitutionalism is a means of keeping reformism bound by Conservative guidelines. Constitutionalism, federalism, and a system of checks and balances have been the chief American Conservative responses to the question of what institutional structures are required to limit properly democratic politics so as to protect their values.

Closely associated with constitutionalism is the rule of law. The rule of law has been an important part of the means by which Conservatives hope to limit democratic politics and curb the dangers and irrationalities they believe to be inherent in the masses under conditions of unrestrained democracy. Conservatives stress the importance of the legal system not being under the immediate and direct influence of temporary, populistic majorities. However, this does not mean they support judicial activism, which in their view gives the courts too much power.

A final, and very important, institutional question with which Conservatism is very concerned in its discussion of the sources of order and disorder in democratic society involves the problem of centralization and decentralization of governmental power. Conservatives, especially in twentieth-century America, have been very apprehensive about the centralization of power by the federal government. They are afraid that such centralization is a danger to the constitutional system.

However, the general Conservative sentiment in favor of a decentralized political system predates the democratic period of Western history; it is not a theme that Conservatives have only recently expressed. In many ways it goes back to the feudal period of Western history and is found in the general aristocratic orientation of Conservative thought. The desire to protect decentralized political structures found perceptive expression in the protests of Justus Möser, the eighteenth-century German Conservative. He saw the centralizing nation state as an enemy of society's natural variety.[26] There is thus nothing novel in the protests of contemporary Conservatives against "big government." However, the Conservative position on this matter requires further analysis.

But before exploring their ideas about political decentralization, it is important to note that Conservative views of democracy do not focus solely upon restraining rash and ill-informed majorities. In the last two decades a number of Conservatives have expressed considerable criticism of liberal elites in the American academic community, the federal bureaucracy, and the news media. On a number of issues, such as on local control of public education at the primary and secondary levels, Conservatives have opposed the above elites in the name of local majorities. Criticism of the so-called "New Class" of liberal, upper-middle-class, university-educated social scientists and government planners who live off of government spending and federal domination of state and local governments has added a "neopopulist" coloring to the "New Right" and the political thinking of individuals like Kevin Phillips. Here the elites are criticized in the name of the masses. This produces a somewhat different attitude than the one usually associated with Conservatism when it comes to comparing elites and ordinary citizens.

However, this newer attitude can be reconciled with the views of the traditionalist Conservative when similar values are under attack. The differences derive from having to rely upon opposing political strategies when liberal elites attack Conservative values, as against cases when populistic majorities endanger such values.

This recent development not only represents a new source of differences among Conservatives, but it also shows the problems Conservatism faces because of its traditional elitist attitudes. The endorsement of many liberal attitudes by so many elite groups in contemporary Western society greatly complicates the traditionalist Conservative's ideas about social and political leadership. It also adds to concern about the direction modern society is heading.

This entire problem is also related to the contemporary debate over political decentralization. What many Conservative leaders face is a political struggle against liberal elites who have a vested interest in federal domination of state and local governments.

PART VI: DECENTRALIZATION AND COMMUNITY

On an institutional basis, a primary Conservative concern of how to achieve a free and orderly society relates to the problem of striking a balance between the centralization and decentralization of political structures. The problem is a difficult one because Conservatives not only stress the theme of decentralization in regard to some political structures and issues, but they also stress the theme of centralization in regard to other political issues. Conservatives argue for a strong national government in order to deal with the problem of domestic factions and to serve in the maintenance of national security in the face of possible foreign threats. One needs to recall at this point the contributions to American Conservatism of Alexander Hamilton and John Adams; these two Federalists stressed the need for strong government to protect people from the more violent and irrational aspects of their natures. A peaceful and orderly society required strong, effective government. Hamilton also argued that development of the nation's economic potential required national leadership and enlightened federal policy.

But at the same time many Conservatives fear the centralization of administrative power by national governments and argue that a properly organized society requires a great deal of administrative and political decentralization. One might wonder how Conservatives can argue for strong government and political centralization at one time and for limited government and political decentralization on other occasions. The clue to reconciling these positions is to recall Madison's statement:

> But what is government itself, but the greatest of all reflections on human nature? If men were angels, no government would be necessary. If angels were to govern men, neither external nor internal controls on government would be necessary. In framing a government, which is to be administered by men over men, the great difficulty lies

in this: You must first enable the government to control the governed; and in the next place, oblige it to control itself.[27]

In addition to constitutionalism American Conservatives have looked to federalism as an institutional solution both to the political dilemma posed by Madison and as a way to combine the best features of political centralization and decentralization. The direction in which Conservatives lean depends upon the political issues, values, and circumstances involved in each case.

When it comes to public order and national security, Conservatives look to a strong federal government. But when it comes to protecting freedom and community values, they argue for political decentralization. American Conservatives, who defend the federal nature of the American political system as originally designed by the Founding Fathers, agree with Alexis de Tocqueville when he writes:

> Granting for an instant that the villages and counties of the United States would be more usefully governed by a remote authority, which they had never seen, than by functionaries taken from the midst of them,—admitting, for the sake of argument, that the country would be more secure, and the resources of society better employed, if the whole administration centered in a single arm, still the *political* advantages which the Americans derive from their system would induce me to prefer it to the contrary plan. It profits me but little after all, that a vigilant authority should protect the tranquility of my pleasures, and constantly avert all dangers from my path, without my care or my concern, if this same authority is the absolute mistress of my liberty and my life, and if it is so monopolizes all the energy of existence, that when it languishes everything languishes around it, that when it sleeps everything must sleep, that when it dies the State itself must perish.[28]

In Tocqueville's statement one can see the kernel of all future

Conservative protests against excessive political and bureaucratic centralization. The Reagan administration represents this viewpoint as it attempts to reverse the centralizing trends of the past fifty years.

However, a challenge to the Conservative's call for a great deal of political decentralization can be constructed even from the standpoint of his own values. Conservatives fear irrational and populistic majorities which they believe often pose a threat to the stability of society and to human freedom. Yet, it is often in local and state areas, where there is a great deal of political and administrative decentralization, where one may find some of the most irrational, dangerous, and populistic majorities. The classic example of this problem can be found in the unjust treatment of American blacks by bigoted white majorities in Southern states and communities that have tried to hide themselves under Conservative constitutional theories and notions of political and administrative decentralization. American Conservatives have, in many cases, failed to come to grips with the problem of how to cope with those who would use their constitutional theories and belief in political decentralization as means to protect social and political practices which repudiate many of the values found in theocentric humanism.

It is important to note that the Conservative support for a decentralized federal system, with special attention being given to local and state governments, owes much to the "traditionalist" Conservative's veneration for the idea of community. Burke writes:

> To be attached to the subdivision, to love the little platoon we belong to in society, is the first principle (the gem as it were) of public affections. It is the first link in the series by which we proceed towards a love of our country and to mankind.[29]

One of the central themes of Conservative disenchantment with modern society has been a protest against the decline of rural community ties and hierarchical and deferential social relationships. Conservatives hold that the strong affective relationships found in community life are essential for an orderly and morally healthy society. They also believe that small, hierarchical communities are essential for the proper development of the moral and emotional life of the individual. T. S. Eliot captures an essential image of the "traditionalist" Conservative's veneration for community life when he writes:

> It is important that a man should feel himself to be, not merely a citizen of a particular nation, but a citizen of a particular part of his country, with local loyalties. These, like loyalty to class, arise out of loyalty to the family. Certainly, an individual may develop the warmest devotion to a place in which he was not born, and to a community with which he has no ancestral ties. But I think we should agree that there would be something artificial, something a little too conscious, about a community of people with strong local feeling, all of whom had come from somewhere else. I think we should say that we must wait for a generation or two for a loyalty which the inhabitants had inherited, and which was not the result of a conscious choice. On the whole, it would appear to be for the best that the great majority of human beings should go on living in the place in which they were born. Family, class, and local loyalty all support each other; and if one of these decays, the others will suffer also.[30]

Conservatives value what they believe to be the security and meaning that stable community relationships provide for the life of the individual. Conservatives generally regard modern society as increasingly disordered, both in terms of social stability and in terms of the meaning to the individual's life, because of the decline of community life. Conservatives have blamed a wide range of causes: the growth of the nation state and its tendency to expand and centralize its power, the industrialization and urbanization of society, the increased mobility of the population, and the influence of the rationalistic spirit on the beliefs and mores which play such a crucial role in rural community relationships.

It is also important to realize that the Conservative's veneration for community is ultimately founded upon a belief in the family as the most important of social units. Family relationships serve as the kernel for community relationships. Much of present-day Conservative criticisms of society and the policies of the federal government center on the decline of traditional family values.

The pessimistic undertone of the Conservative theory about community and what has happened to it and traditional family bonds in modern society is that it is difficult to see how to restore the kind of community relationships and family ties necessary for a good society once these are damaged.

PART VII: CONSERVATIVE VIEWS ON PROPERTY AND THE DIVISION OF LABOR

No study of the Conservative's view of the sources of order for society would be complete without dealing with his attitudes toward property and the division of labor. Conservatives argue that property is essential to human freedom, the family, and social stability. Rossiter holds:

> Property makes it possible for man to be free. Independence and privacy can never be enjoyed by one who must rely on other persons or agencies—especially government—for food, shelter, and material comforts. Property gives him a place on which to stand and make free choices; it grants him a sphere in which he may ignore the state. Property is the most important single technique for the diffusion of economic power. Property is essential to the existence of the family, the natural unit of society. Property provides the main incentive for productive work. Human nature being what it is and always will be, the

desire to acquire and hold property is essential to progress. Finally, property is a powerful conservative agent, giving support and substance to that temperament which helps to stabilize society.[31]

However, while Conservatives will forever defend private property against socialist expropriation, they do not always agree on what kind of private property it is they are defending. Close examination of the Conservative position will show that it is really dominated by two different views of property and the division of labor. On the one hand there is the "traditionalist" view, which is basically precapitalistic in orientation. There is also the "libertarian" view, which is highly capitalistic in outlook.

The Conservative's defense of property constitutes one of his basic institutional beliefs about the proper ordering of society. Historically, the "traditionalist" Conservative defense of landed property and the rights and obligations entailed by such holdings has been strongly aristocratic and agrarian in orientation. The position also owes much to the Conservative veneration of the extended family. Burke writes:

> The power of perpetuating our property in our families is one of the most valuable and interesting circumstances belonging to it, and that which tends the most to the perpetuation of society itself. It makes our weaknesses subservient to our virtue; it grafts benevolence even upon avarice. The possessors of family wealth, and of the distinction which attends hereditary possession (as most concerned in it), are the natural securities for this transmission.[32]

The "traditionalist" Conservative position maintains that a society based on long-established family landholdings makes possible the kind of environment which aids in the development of well-rounded individuals who can make the most of human freedom. Those supporting this position argue that family landholdings carry with them the kind of obligations and duties which are vital for the development of the right kind of citizens. Those who own such land not only have an obligation to preserve their family but also have obligations to care for the larger community. The kind of property valued by these Conservatives stands in great contrast to the property relationships dominant in contemporary Western society. This view of property has its grounding in the context of a division of labor that is both rural and rather simple in nature.

This view of property has its basis in a society where the simple division of labor gives rise to what some authors term "hard property." This kind of property is such that the individual has very direct and total relationship toward it. In the case of the landed property held by a family, the individuals have a very direct, concrete, and lasting relationship with the land. Karl Mannheim captures the essence of this view of property in his study of early German Conservatism:

> The peculiar nature of conservative concreteness is perhaps hardly more clearly to be seen than in its concept of *property*, as contrasted with the ordinary modern bourgeois idea of it. In this connection there is a very interesting essay of Möser's in which he traces the gradual disappearance of the old attitude towards property and compares it with the modern concept of property which had already begun to show its influence in his own time. In his essay *"Von dem echten Eigentum"* he shows that the old "genuine property" was bound up with its owner in an entirely different way from property today. Before, there was a peculiarly vital, reciprocal relationship between property and its owner. Property in its old "genuine" sense carried with it certain privileges for its owner—for instance, it gave him a voice in affairs of state, the right to hunt, to become a member of a jury. Thus it was closely bound up with his personal honour and so in a sense *"inalienable."*[33]

This kind of property is quite different from the kind of "soft" property which dominates advanced industrial society. This kind of property is a direct part of the owner's daily existence; it does not exist on paper or lie stored away in a vault. The "traditionalist" view must regard the human relationships based on such "soft" property relationships as indirect and "abstract."

This view of property can better be understood by considering what it has to say about the conditions of labor in rural society as opposed to an industrial society. The "traditionalist" Conservative tends to idealize the life of the medieval craftsman and the relationship the craftsman had to what he created, while being quite concerned about the kind of life of the industrial worker and the relationship he has to what he creates.

The "traditionalist" view sees modern industrial society as inherently disordered because of its complex division of labor and "abstract" property relationships. This view holds that in a more simple society the individual is able to understand his place in and contribution to society. Life is able to have meaning for the individual in such a society. The "traditionalist" view holds that in a society based on a very complex division of labor, where "soft" property relationships replace "hard" property relationships, the individual finds society too complex to understand. The individual cannot understand his place in modern society or the nature of his contribution to society; his self-esteem suffers, and his life appears meaningless in the face of such incomprehensible complexity. Human relationships appear abstract and alien in such a society when compared to the concrete human relations found in a society based on "hard" property. What is more, according to this view the political activity of individuals and groups, viewing the complex society from only the perspective of small portions of the over-all division of labor, tends to become more irrational and contradictory as the division of labor becomes more complex. The cognitive simplicity that is able to function in a simple society cannot function in a

complex society. As the division of labor increases, and society becomes more complex, political rationality becomes
more difficult.

Interestingly enough, the "traditionalist" Conservative
view of property leads to a critique of modern industrial society that shares much in common with the critique of capitalist society advanced by the socialist tradition of thought.
As Karl Mannheim points out in regard to Conservative
thought:

> For Hegel the essence of property is that "I make a thing
> the vehicle of my will," and "the rationale of property con-
> sists, not in that it satisfies our needs, but in that it helps
> personality become something more than mere subjectiv-
> ity." It is also interesting to note here something which we
> shall have occasion to observe again later—how the Left
> opposition to bourgeois capitalist thought learns from the
> Right opposition to bourgeois thought. The abstractness of
> human relationships under capitalism which is constantly
> emphasized by Marx and his followers was originally the
> discovery of observers from the conservative camp.[34]

But the "traditionalist" Conservative critique of modern society differs from the socialist critique in that it is aimed at
industrial society per se, while the socialist critique is directed
against a particular form of industrial society: capitalism.

However, there is another Conservative view of property
and the division of labor which looks at industrial society,
especially the capitalist form, in a much more favorable light.
The "libertarian" Conservative view rests upon veneration
for the kind of property and property relationships of the private entrepreneur. Whereas the "traditionalist" view is rural
in orientation, the "libertarian" position is industrial. While
the "traditionalist" Conservative views ownership in family
terms, the "libertarian" Conservative conceives of ownership
as being held by individuals. One view represents continuing
unease and distrust of industrial and capitalist society, while
the other view shows acceptance of industrial society and a

desire to defend capitalism. The "libertarian" Conservative view of property and the division of labor shows us the great influence of classical liberal thought on the thinking of many contemporary Conservatives. The works of William Graham Sumner, Ludwig von Mises, Friedrick Hayek, and Milton Friedman are very important in this context. The "libertarian" view rests upon the conceptualization of a basically laissez-faire economic system. The Conservatives who adhere to this view are thus committed to defending eighteenth- and nineteenth-century liberal beliefs in the right to private property and a free-market economy against twentieth-century reform liberalism.

The "libertarian" Conservative argues that the "traditionalist" view is guilty of romanticizing fedual and rural society. He argues that the "traditionalist" Conservative overlooks the disadvantages of rural society. By increasing the division of labor industrial society increases the material base of society and makes possible a higher level of civilization. The "libertarian" position holds that industrial society makes possible greater diversity and potential for the life of the individual. Also, the industrialization of society, at least in terms of the potentials it offers for the individual, constitutes a significant step forward in human history. The "libertarian" Conservatives too have great admiration for what they regard as the creative energy of the private entrepreneur and for the kinds of freedoms to be found in capitalist society. They are likely to agree with the defense of industrial capitalism advanced by Ludwig von Mises in his *Human Action*. There Mises reminds the romanticizers of rural society about the centuries of rural poverty, ignorance, disease, and human degradation found in the preindustrial order. In the case of Jefferson's yeoman farmer, and certainly in the view of the owners of large plantations, rural life has many virtues. But to consider only the costs of industrialization, without recalling the miseries of preindustrial society, is likely to produce an imbalanced judgment of the two societies.

It is easy to understand the problem that the Conservative

thinker faces when he is asked about the process of industrializing the so-called "underdeveloped" nations of the world. One line of Conservative thought warns such nations about the costs of industrialization, while another school of thought urges that industrialization proceed. Most Conservatives fall somewhere in between these two opposing views; they want the best of both worlds: they want the developing nations to follow the American model of industrial capitalism while avoiding the damage done to traditional values in the American experiment. Just how this is to be done is never made clear.

However, the two views do share some things in common. Both venerate what is called "hard property," the property of the farmer or the property of the private entrepreneur. Both views are critical of the property of large corporations, which they regard as "soft property." The two positions are often conveniently, and uncritically, blended together in the thinking of individual Conservatives who, in contemporary politics, try to rally around the defense of the property of the small farmer and small businessman. Most importantly, both views face a similar historical problem. The kind of property valued by each position is endangered by the economic evolution of modern society. The defenders of the "traditionalist" position have, since the very beginning of the industrial revolution in the West, been aware of the fact that modern society is moving in a direction away from honoring their kind of property. And many defenders of the "libertarian" view (one may think here of Joseph Schumpeter's veneration for the pioneer industrialists and his analysis of capitalism's evolution) have come to the realization that the evolution of corporate capitalism works against their kind of property. One needs to consider here how often corporate elites support collectivist economic policies which are opposed by small farmers and small businessmen. Both views lead the Conservative to be critical of modern society.

However, despite what the two Conservative views share in common, it is impossible to forget the points where they are at odds. The differences between the two add considerable tension to Conservative thought and threaten its internal unity. What helps to hold Conservatism together on the subject of property is that such theoretical differences seem less important when one encounters the attack launched upon both of them by liberal and socialist movements in the twentieth century. Both Conservative views of property are criticized by contemporary liberals and socialists in the name of equality. It is precisely on this issue where one can find crucial agreement between both schools of Conservative thought regarding property: both views defend considerable inequalities in the distribution of property, income, and wealth.

Conservatives view inequality in the distribution of property as the natural consequence of allowing people to be free. They agree with John C. Calhoun's argument:

> Now, as individuals differ greatly from each other in intelligence, sagacity, energy, perseverance, skill, habits of industry and economy, physical power, position and opportunity—the necessary effect of leaving all free to exert themselves to better their condition must be a corresponding inequality between those who may possess these qualities and advantages in a high degree and those who may be deficient in them.[35]

Economic inequality is unavoidable in a free society.

Conservative economic thought begins with a belief in the natural inequalities existing between individuals and the importance of allowing individuals considerable freedom in trying to improve the conditions of their lives. Calhoun presents the classic Conservative argument on this subject as he discusses the relationship between liberty and equality:

> That they are united to a certain extent, and that equality of citizens, in the eyes of the law, is essential to liberty in a popular government is conceded. But to go further and make equality of *condition* essential to liberty would be to destroy both liberty and progress. The reason is that

inequality of condition, while it is a necessary consequence of liberty, is at the same time indispensable to progress. In order to understand why this is so, it is necessary to bear in mind that the mainspring to progress is the desire of individuals to better their condition, and that the strongest impulse which can be given to it is to leave individuals free to exert themselves in the manner they may deem best for that purpose, as far at least as it can be done consistently with the ends for which government is ordained, and to secure to all the fruits of their exertions.[36]

Conservatives see personal freedom, initiative, and the opportunity to acquire private property for oneself and one's family as essential to human progress and the development of better standards of living. For these reasons a majority of contemporary Conservatives have accepted the "libertarian" view of property and are willing to defend industrial capitalism, despite "traditionalist" reservations. The best recent example of a Conservative's defense of basing an economic system on private property and free-market ground rules is found in George Gilder's *Wealth and Poverty* (New York: Basic Books, 1981).

The acceptance of such an economic system has important consequences for Conservative political thinking, which has much in common with nineteenth-century liberal ideas about the proper role of government in society. Just as important, it means accepting the inevitability of class differences and conflict within society. One need only recall Madison's observation in *Federalist Paper* No. 10 that factions are born from economic differences existing between various groups in society:

> The diversity in the faculties of men, from which the rights of property originate, is not less an insuperable obstacle to an uniformity of interests. The protection of those faculties is the first object of government. From the protection of different and unequal faculties of acquiring property, the possession of different degrees and kinds of

property immediately results; and from the influence of these on the sentiments and views of the respective proprietors, ensues a division of the society into different interests and parties.

The latent causes of faction are thus sown in the nature of man; and we see them everywhere brought into different degrees of activity, according to the different circumstances of civil society.[37]

Like Madison, most Conservatives see factionalism as posing great dangers to society, but are committed to a belief in private property which makes factions inevitable. They see the communist solution to the problem of factions by abolishing private property as, to use Madison's words, a "remedy which is worse than the disease." Like Madison, they wish to support cultural and institutional means to limit the damage that factions and social classes can do to each other and society.

The conclusions to be drawn from what Conservatism has to say about the sources of order and disorder in society give plenty of reason to be concerned about the prospects for modern society. Conservative theory suggests that conditions necessary for a well-ordered society have been damaged. The right kind of religious and moral traditions, cultural life, aristocratic leadership, political decentralization, and community life have, in the Conservative's eyes, received considerable setbacks in modern society. Conservative theory about order in society requires conditions that the industrialization, secularization, administrative centralization, and rationalization of modern society have endangered. Given their position about the sources of order for society, it is not surprising that Conservatives are sometimes pessimistic about how to restore order to modern society. For if Conservative theory is correct, then modern society is in serious trouble.

Conservatives need somehow to convince contemporary elites and popular majorities of the need to return to older traditions and values, to support prudent reforms in order to prevent revolution, to decentralize the political and administrative life of the country, to rebuild the sense of community, and to rekindle the quest for excellence in individual endeavors. The bottom line of their analysis of the disorders found in modern society revolves around the issue of leadership in a democratic society. Their indictment of the liberal leadership found in Western societies in recent decades deplores the extent to which various elites have abandoned, and led the general public to abandon, important Conservative values essential to an orderly, free, and morally healthy society. For Conservatives the future course of modern society depends upon their ability to lead their countries in directions quite different from where they have been moving.

6. The Relationship between Theoretical and Practical Reason in Conservative Thought

One of the central themes of Conservative thought is that a balance must be struck betwen theoretical and practical reason in thinking about politics. On the one hand the Conservative holds that there are certain religious, metaphysical, and moral truths about God, man, and the universe which must be the objects of theoretical reason and must not be lost sight of in thinking about political questions. Yet at the same time they also hold that the complexities of the political world are such that thinking about specific political problems must be guided by empirical and pragmatic considerations. The Conservative holds that the proper kind of thinking about politics requires the successful relating of theoretical and practical modes of reasoning. The issue to be dealt with now concerns the problems that Conservatism faces in the contemporary world in trying to fulfill this demand.

One of the greatest problems facing Conservatism is to show how its religious beliefs (its Cosmological principle) and its moral principles (found in its theocentric humanism and natural law theory) relate to specific political issues. This is not an easy task, for it is not always clear just what course of political action is dictated by the Conservative's religious and moral principles. There are many individuals whose religious beliefs, moral values, and cultural preferences are Conservative, but whose political views are liberal. Conservatives have no monopoly on religious orthodoxy and adherence to traditional moral and cultural values. There are many liberals who believe in God, order their personal lives according to very strict moral principles, and are concerned about the decline of cultural standards.

On top of this, Conservatives often disagree among themselves as to the political implications of their general religious and moral principles. The political differences between "traditionalist" and "libertarian" Conservatives point to the problems of moving from the abstract to the concrete. This not only creates difficulty for the internal harmony of Conservative thought but also calls into question whether contemporary Conservatism has successfully related its theoretical and practical modes of reasoning.

One needs to ask just why it is that Conservatism would face this problem of relating its theoretical and practical reasoning, of having different Conservatives coming to opposing political conclusions while employing similar principles. There are two important features of Conservative thought that help to explain the existence of this problem in the first place.

The first reason lies in the rejection of doctrinaire, programmatic political thinking. Conservatives oppose the kind of thinking by which political programs are logically deduced from a set of general principles, by which all political questions are resolved by reference to theory. For any individual Conservative to declare that his political proposals are *the* Conservative program, the only program that can be justified and deduced from Conservative principles, would violate the general warning against political rationalism.

This is not to say that Conservatives never advance political programs as solutions to various problems. The Reagan administration clearly supports a number of programs as necessary for a stronger country. There is a Conservative agenda for the 1980s which calls for restraining the growth of federal spending, tax cuts, reducing the scope of government regulations, decentralizing political structures, and expanding American military strength. While some of this involves new programs, much of it simply involves modifying existing programs. Regardless of the theoretical inspiration for such policies, and regardless of the desirability of trying to tie these programs together in a systematic way in order to avoid the charge of being incoherent and lacking over-all objectives, these proposals are not an ideological blueprint for completely restructuring American society. Despite the boasts of those Reagan supporters who speak of a "conservative revolution" and the cries of his critics who think he is tearing apart a system they helped to create, the accomplishment of most of Reagan's goals would still leave basic features of the present system intact. There would be important changes in the direction of the country, desirable from the standpoint of Conservatives, but the society would not be radically transformed. Some social programs may be cut, but the total amount of federal spending for social programs would still be in the hundreds of billions of dollars. The country would be left with a Conservative welfare state as opposed to a liberal welfare state.

The Reagan administration may well succeed in having the issues of the day debated on its terms, for the rhetorical challenge to American liberalism posed by Reagan is considerable. However, the Reagan programs are not programmatic in the tradition of the more radical political parties of Europe, where total programs for social change may be found. And as one examines the Reagan proposals, one can see Conservatives disagreeing among themselves as to their content and whether they go too far or not far enough in changing the direction of the country.

The second source of disagreement between Conservatives may be found in the pluralist nature of their value system. Because there are no clear-cut formulae governing the multitude of their values, individual Conservatives, when dealing with specific political questions, are free to choose and give the greatest stress to different values and principles, hence the disagreements between so many of them on specific political issues. This also produces differences as to which public issues ought to receive the greatest attention.

One of the major disagreements found in American Conservativism in the 1980s involves the conflicting demands made on the Reagan administration by those who believe that resolution of economic problems facing the nation has the highest priority as opposed to those who want social issues to come first. The first group involves those "libertarian" Conservatives influenced by laissez-faire liberalism. These individuals believe that saving the country involves reducing the tax burden, encouraging individual initiative and saving, restraining the growth of federal spending, and reducing government regulation of business. Working with this group are those Conservatives who desire a more decentralized federal system.

The second group involves Conservatives inspired by "traditionalist" religious beliefs and values. These individuals believe saving the country requires that something be done about the growing secularization of the society, abortion, pornography, and the decline of traditional family values. Much to the consternation of several "New Right" religious groups, the Reagan administration, thus far, has paid much more attention to the demands of the first group.

Both groups invoke theoretical principles important to Conservatism, but they cannot agree as to which issues should have priority. What is more, the proposals of the two groups are not always consistent. One cannot diminish the impact of the federal government on the life of the individual by passing a constitutional amendment to outlaw abortion. The differences between these two groups are, in some respects, a replay of some of the earlier differences between the "libertarian" and "traditionalist" schools of thought. But the conflict is also different for at least three reasons.

First of all, the present debate takes place at a time when Conservatism is quite strong in the country and has won a number of important victories, the most important being the election of Ronald Reagan as president. Conservatives must now deal with questions about priorities while trying to govern and hold on to political power in a democratic society. The earlier debates took place under very different political circumstances. Second, the advocates of each side in the present debate have received much more publicity than the spokesmen of a decade ago. Advocates of supply-side economics and leaders of the religious "New Right" have carried the logic of their positions so far that some of the surviving spokesmen of the older "libertarian" and "traditionalist" positions have called for a little moderation. Third, participants in the current controversy have developed a much stronger organizational base from which to advance their positions.

The relationship between theoretical and practical reason in Conservative thought is thus very diverse, ambiguous, and open to a variety of differing interpretations. From the standpoint of the person who demands more coherence in the relationship between theory and practice, Conservatism fails to establish a clear and direct relation between the two. The criticism can be made that contemporary Conservatives fail to live up to their own demand that the two be closely related in political thinking. However, before the validity of this criticism can be determined, the Conservative position on the matter must be examined in greater detail.

The Conservative position concerning the relationship between the theoretical and practical modes of political thought can be better understood by examining what C. E. Lindblom has to say about how values should be treated in the policy-making process. Lindblom shares with many Conservatives a common rejection of the rationalist mode of political thinking. His discussion of disjointed incrementalism in policy formation not only captures the essence of the Conservative critique of rationalist political thought but also contains important beliefs about how values (and the general principles which are the objects of theoretical reason) should be treated in dealing with practical political questions.

According to the pristine rationalist ideal four steps should take place in relating values to practical political questions:

(1) values are arranged in preferential order—a systematic theory of ethics is devised—all values are put in their proper rank;

(2) the social situation is analyzed, and all the technically possible alternatives are set forth;

(3) those established alternatives are then evaluated in terms of the already established preferential scale of values in order to determine the costs and benefits of each alternative;

(4) a decision is then made on the basis of which alternative will bring us closer to the realization of the highest values found in the elaborated system of values.

It is important to keep in mind that in the rationalist ideal steps (3) and (4) do not take place until steps (1) and (2) have been completed.

What Lindblom does is to call into question the wisdom of step (1) in the rationalist ideal and its relationship to the other steps in the process. He argues that step (1) is impossible and does not accurately reflect the role of values in the policy-making process.[1] He holds that values have varying marginal utility under different circumstances and that preferences often can and should change as these values have been satisfied to various degrees. Lindblom holds that the rationalist method of dealing with value questions in policy formation overlooks the fact that while value x may be preferred to value y in some kind of hypothetical and original ranking of values, x may not be preferred to y in other situations where its preference might mean a great sacrifice of yet other values.

The rationalist ideal, by step (1), intends to provide an a priori picture of what policy aims should be and seeks to direct the evaluation of specific policy alternatives. Lindblom's criticism of this is that it makes no sense to rank all of one's goals without measuring their costs, but such costs cannot always be known on an a priori basis.[2] An original ranking of value preferences would have to answer the question of costs in advance. Step (1) would require a superhuman feat of intuition and comprehension in which one is able to exhaust conceptually all the possible relationships among the different marginal aspects of values and measure all the marginal costs of accepting one value over another. Lindblom's primary objection to the rationalist ideal is thus epistemological in nature.

The Reagan programs should thus be understood in incremental terms, which is in keeping with the spirit of Conservative reformism. This is not to deny that important changes are being advocated. But the Reagan proposals are not a rationalistic blueprint for revolutionary transformation of American society.

Given the common ground that exists between Lindblom and Conservative critics of rationalist thought, it thus becomes easier to understand certain basic features of Conservative moral theory and the nature of the relationship that Conservatives believe should hold between theoretical and practical reasoning in politics. First of all, it is now easier to understand a difficult problem facing Conservative moral theory. While Conservatives believe in an absolute moral ordering to the universe and adhere to a natural-law theory, there has always been an embarrassing ambiguity in Conservative thought about the relative value and exact relationship among virtue, order, and liberty. It should now be apparent that this ambiguity is inevitable in Conservative thought because of its rejection of the idea that the exact nature of the relationship among the three values (as well as their relative merits) can be clearly spelled out in terms of any rationalistic formula. For a Conservative to try to formalize the relationship among the three values and to rank them in a priori fashion so that they could then serve as universal guidelines in policy formation would be to violate what other Conservatives have said against such a procedure. This would involve trying to determine in advance what simply cannot be known in advance.

While Conservatives are motivated by general values and committed to numerous theoretical positions, they do not endorse specific policies without considering their practical consequences. Even the Reagan administration's endorsement of supply-side economics, while inspired by the ideas of laissez-faire liberalism, rests upon an assessment (not shared by all Conservatives) of the practical consequences of such policies.

An important notion colors the relationship that Conservatives maintain should exist between theoretical and practical reasoning in politics. Conservatives hold that what man believes he has learned from theoretical speculation, what he believes about his most important values and principles, should only be related to political action in a spirit of moderation and compromise. Moderation and compromise are perceived as important to a sound relationship between theory and practice because of the Conservative's belief in the limitations of human reason (reflected in man's inability to engage successfully in rationalistic ranking of all values) and the complexity and ever-changing nature of political circumstances.

Thus, while Conservatives argue that virtue ought to be the pursuit of every individual, they do not conclude that it should be the practical political policy of the state to force all men to live a virtuous life. The Conservative's emphasis on compromise and moderation leads him to hold that, in Burke's words:

> It is better to cherish virtue and humanity, by leaving much to free will, even with some loss to the object, than to attempt to make men mere machines and instruments

of a political benevolence. The world on the whole will gain by a liberty, without which virtue cannot exist.[3]

The position of Burke on this matter has much in common with the position of Thomas Aquinas that there is a natural law, but it would not be wise to devise human law so as to try to forbid all that is forbidden by the natural law. The basic moderation of Aquinas' position can be seen in his statement:

> . . . law is framed as a rule or measure of human acts. Now a measure should be homogeneous with that which it measures, as stated in *Metaphysics* x. text. 3, 4 [Aristotle], since different things are measured by different measures. Wherefore laws imposed on men should also be in keeping with their condition, for, as Isodore says, law should be "possible both according to nature, and according to the customs of the country." . . .
>
> Now human law is framed for a number of human beings, the majority of whom are not perfect in virtue. Wherefore human laws do not forbid all vices from which the virtuous abstain, but only the more grievous vices from which it is possible for the majority to abstain; and chiefly those that are to the hurt of others, without the prohibition of which human society could not be maintained: thus human law prohibits murder, theft, and suchlike. . . .
>
> The purpose of human law is to lead men to virtue, not suddenly, but gradually. Wherefore it does not lay upon the multitude of imperfect men the burdens of those who are already virtuous, viz., that they should abstain from all evil.[4]

The position of Aquinas here, and it is one shared by most Conservatives, is that man's nature is such that human existence cannot directly be structured according to the discoveries of man's theoretical reasoning. This position also implies tolerance of human shortcomings. Indeed, it is this spirit of tolerance, this reluctance to force mankind into an ideological strait jacket, that helps to distinguish a true Conservative from the left-wing revolutionary (who is motivated by a vision of an ideal society of the future) and the right-wing reactionary (who is motivated by a mythical view of a distant golden age).

This does not mean that Conservatives ignore their moral values when making recommendations about the content of public law. They believe that law should promote virtue along with freedom and order; they do not accept the argument of so many civil libertarians that law should somehow be neutral regarding moral values, for they see such a demand as impossible. The real problem for Conservatism concerns how far it is prudent to go in upholding moral standards while avoiding an impossible and politically unwise attempt to make the law a weapon against every imaginable act of wrongdoing. While their general principles lead them to hold that abortion, pornography, and homosexuality are morally wrong, Conservatives disagree among themselves as to how far the law should go regarding such activities. Here is where it becomes difficult to relate the Conservative's moral ideals to his practical concerns about the content of public law. One must somehow balance concern for virtue with a recognition of human imperfectibility and the limits on what government is capable of doing. It also means trying to reconcile "traditionalist" and "libertarian" values and perspectives.

Conservatives are critical of rationalistic political thinking because they believe that the rationalist perceives the relationship between theoretical and practical reason in terms of a one-way street. The rationalist adapts his practical political thinking to his theoretical reasoning in terms of adjusting means to ends. The Conservative, however, also believes that it is sometimes necessary to adjust one's ends according to the means available. The Conservative is thus willing to compromise in the pursuit of his goals and even adjust his goals so as to be capable of functioning in an imperfect realm of existence.

It is a common contemporary criticism of their critique of rationalistic political thought that Conservatives are attacking a straw man and that the attack on liberalism for being rationalistic is directed toward thinkers of an era long past. But this criticism is really untrue. One need only think of John Rawls' *A Theory of Justice* in order to see that what Conservatives mean by rationalistic political thinking is far from dead. Rawls' whole theory, which serves as a brilliant justification for some of the most crucial statements of liberal political theory, rests upon imagining what principles rational and self-interested individuals would choose by which to order society if they existed in a hypothetical and initial condition of equality where man's most important political principles are to be chosen on an a priori basis. Rawls' theory represents the perfect point of intersection between rationalistic and liberal political thought. Rawls' whole theory rests upon what was earlier termed as step (1) of the rationalist ideal of how values should be related to policy formation.

There is also a form of political rationalism on the right of the political spectrum. Advocates of anarchocapitalism, who believe highways, police, and armies should be run by private corporations, dogmatize the Conservative belief in private property. Some religious fundamentalists, forgetting the points made by Aquinas and Burke about there being limits as to how far the law may go in protecting moral values, dogmatize Conservative ideas about natural law. Such right-wing political rationalism, while motivated by important Conservative principles, violates Conservative warnings against doctrinaire political thinking. Such groups are committed to the kind of programs, ranging from the abolition of all government regulation of business to the passing of a Constitutional amendment banning abortions, which would radically alter American society and the relationship between the government and the governed.

Rather than relying on abstract reasoning as a guide in political thinking, the Conservative is more likely to rely upon prudence. But what should guide the operation of prudence? How can prudence show men how to adapt important values to political circumstances? And how can prudence show men how to modify their political objectives in the light of these circumstances? In answering these essential questions about the relationship between theoretical and practical political reasoning, the Conservative will turn to history. Historical experience is what Conservatives turn to in relating theoretical and practical concerns. History is viewed as what can help determine what are or are not wise political proposals. Clinton Rossiter pursues this idea of history as man's political educator in detail:

> History, in any case, is man's most reliable teacher. It is not "bunk," not a pack of tricks played on the dead by the living or on the living by the dead. It is a mirror in which each nation can find an honest image, a book in which it can read the awesome truth. The nature and capacities of man, the purposes and dangers of government, the origins and limits of change—we learn these things best, the Conservative insists, by studying the past. Without the teachings of men and events, without the traditions that institutionalize these teachings, what resources could we draw upon in the struggle for civilized survival?[5]

Rossiter's point helps one to understand why tradition and custom are so important to Conservatives.

The Conservative believes that tradition and custom can often represent the collective wisdom of man's historical experience. This also helps one to understand why a decline in traditional beliefs and ways of doing things so undermines the Conservative's attempt to relate theory and practice by the use of prudence. Stanley Parry captures the essence of this problem which modernity creates for Conservative thinking:

> Reason operates effectively in its own right only when it moves within the context of a healthy tradition. But in Burke this leads only to a defense of tradition against rationalistic forms of reason. He never had cause to examine

the principle of limitation from another aspect: What is the function of reason when the tradition is sick? When the tradition offers no context for reason, what then are the limits of reason? The Burkean formulation, therefore, is inadequate because it is an *ad hoc* formulation whose terms were dictated by the problem of defending tradition as yet healthy.[6]

Not only does modernity, in its assault upon tradition, undermine effective political reason, but the Conservative also suggests that it damages conditions necessary for responsible moral behavior. Burke argues:

> Prejudice is of ready application in the emergency; it previously engages the mind in a steady course of wisdom and virtue, and does not leave the man hesitating in the moment of decision, sceptical, puzzled, and unresolved. Prejudice renders a man's virtue his habit; and not a series of unconnected acts. Through just prejudice, his duty becomes part of his nature.[7]

But when tradition and prejudice begin to crumble, man then, according to the Conservative, loses his sense of direction, and the possibility of successfully relating general moral concerns and practical political objectives becomes increasingly doubtful.

Having examined in greater detail what Conservatism has to say about the relationship between theoretical and practical reason, it is necessary to evaluate the criticisms which hold that contemporary Conservatives fail to live up to their own position on this matter. Simply because various Conservatives may use common principles and still arrive at different practical conclusions does not mean that their position is incoherent as far as relating theoretical and practical reason. There is nothing unusual in having the adherents of a political theory deriving different practical conclusions from a common set of principles. Among liberals, marxists, and utilitarians one may find similar disagreements about practical political proposals. The open, even ambiguous, relationship that Conservatives believe should exist between theoretical and practical reasoning in politics only appears absurd and completely incoherent if one is judging it in terms of the rationalistic position which holds that the relationship can be formulated and spelled out on an a priori basis.

However, while the problem of having different Conservatives using the same principles to justify very different kinds of political policies may not be used to prove that the relationship between theoretical and practical reason in Conservative thought is completely incoherent, it can serve as the basis for doubting the internal harmony of Conservative political thought and can lead one to wonder what is the exact political meaning of Conservative thought in the twentieth century. This is a problem that will be considered in more detail in the conclusion of this study, where the difficult position of Conservatism vis-à-vis modern society will be examined.

There is, however, another and much more difficult problem facing contemporary Conservative thought in terms of its capacity to live up to its own demands about the successful relating of theoretical and practical modes of reason in politics. As already pointed out, the Conservative believes that it is sometimes necessary to compromise general theoretical principles and prudentially adjust one's ends to the available means. The crucial assumption behind all this is the belief that the process of prudentially adjusting goals to available political means and circumstances will only result in the tactical compromise of theoretical concerns in such a way that those concerns are not betrayed. The compromising of theoretical concerns is not intended by the Conservative to be the selling out of basic values and principles; it is expected to be the process by which one is able to see that those goals, even if they must be prudentially adjusted to circumstances, are still realized to a considerable extent.

In a fundamentally Conservative society this assumption

is easy to make and is usually quite true. In such a society one encounters "natural Conservatism," and the problem of relating theoretical and practical reason does not appear very difficult. Modern society, however, creates considerable difficulty for Conservatism in regard to this matter. Modernity entails a general environment that is incompatible with many Conservative values and principles. While the contemporary Conservative is willing to compromise so as to adapt many of his ends to the means and circumstances available in modern society, it may be difficult to distinguish prudent compromise from betrayal of basic values and concerns. The successful relating of theoretical and practical modes of reasoning becomes more difficult for the Conservative when electoral necessities force him away from his real preferences. There is little guarantee that prudential compromise in modern society will result in the general honoring of basic Conservative values. In the context of modern society many Conservative principles appear very remote, abstract, and extremely difficult to relate to practical political questions. Modernity obscures, makes more difficult, the successful relating of theoretical and practical reason in Conservative thought.

Moderation and compromise, which the Conservative thinks should guide the relationship between theoretical and practical reason, can have dubious consequences for the Conservative facing a social order which has come under liberal influence. The Conservative spirit of compromise faces a crucial problem inherent in the requirements of persuasion in a liberal society. In order to persuade others, an individual must appeal to at least some of the basic premises of those he attempts to persuade. A Conservative winds up being forced to put many of his political proposals in terms that will appeal to liberals. Thus one encounters the difficulty of distinguishing many Conservative economic and political positions from the positions found in different forms of liberal thought. What the individual Conservative thinker does not unconsciously absorb from the dominant forms of liberal thought he is often forced to make use of in his political and economic proposals.

Part of the problem in all this is due to the common ground that Conservative thought shares with liberalism. Conservative and liberal thought intersect at many points. American Conservatives are especially influenced by classical liberal notions of economic freedom. It is not surprising that many of the most important reform ideas (such as the negative income tax, the voucher plan for education, and a variety of proposals for limiting government spending and taxation) Conservatives support or advance for modifying the existing welfare state have been formulated by Milton Friedman, a classical liberal economic thinker. This creates a problem of philosophical identity for the American Conservative and further complicates the relationship between theoretical and practical reason in Conservative thought. The practical political reasoning of many contemporary Conservatives is shaped by the theoretical perspective of laissez-faire liberalism.

The most recent case of such influence lies in the impact of supply-side economic theory on American Conservatism and the Reagan administration. In constructing so much of its domestic policies on the basis of this theory, the Reagan administration has risked much, while downplaying the considerable doubts that a number of Conservatives have about the theory. There is considerable irony in the fact that Conservatives, when advancing alternatives to contemporary liberalism, owe so much to other dimensions of liberal thinking.

This raises again the problem of defining the nature of contemporary Conservatism. The full extent of the difficulty facing Conservative thought on this score can better be seen by more closely examining the general position of Conservatism vis-à-vis modern society.

Conclusion:
Conservatism and Modernity

Any attempt to sum up the meaning of Conservative thought must come to grips with the tension between Conservatism and modern society. While Conservatism by no means rejects all aspects of modernity, the clearest insights into the nature of Conservative thought come through examination of its ongoing critique of crucial underpinnings of modern Western society. The development of Conservative thought in the last three hundred years has taken place in a context in which individual Conservatives have had to combat the evolution of modern thought along secular, rationalist, positivist, liberal, and socialist lines. In some cases the thinking of individual Conservatives owes much to these different systems of thought. This can be seen in the impact of different forms of liberalism on the political and economic thinking of Conservatives. However, while Conservatives have borrowed much from liberal thought, in regard to their basic philosophical orientation they have remained opposed to liberalism and the other dominant forms of modern thought.

While it is an old, frequently misleading, and unfair, rhetorical ploy to label Conservatives as reactionaries, the accusation can sometimes be revealing. The charge that Conservative thought is in a sense reactionary, when that term is

177

stripped of its pejorative connotations, has some portion of truth to it and reveals much about both the Conservative and his critics. For the charge captures the underlying Conservative hostility to and rejection of what much of modernity has come to stand for, as well as the embracing of modernity by most of those making the charge against Conservatives.

Modernity may be understood in terms of the ongoing development of several interrelated and mutually reinforcing phenomena. First, there is the secularization of human life and man's way of thinking about the universe and himself. Second, there is the rationalization (as understood by Weber and Mannheim) of human existence both in terms of how men live and how they think. Third, there is the industrialization of first Western society and then its spread to the rest of the world. Fourth, there is the great centralization of power in the hands of nation states. Fifth, there is the decline of community. Finally, thanks in a large measure to the above developments, there is the decline of traditional religious, moral, cultural, and political values. These phenomena combined have helped to create a society in which the Conservative can never feel completely at home.

Such a society is fundamentally different from the kind of society based on a God-centered mode of living and thinking, a society which highly values "mystery" and views as sacred and irreducible the nonrational aspects of man's existence. Contemporary society daily assaults values crucial to the Conservative's conception of the good society. Modernity makes impossible a society where "natural Conservatism" can flourish and creates what must be regarded as a permanent state of alienation between the Conservative and his society. This helps to account for many of the earlier mentioned paradoxes and difficulties one encounters in examining Conservative thought. According to the vulgar interpretation of Conservative thought, Conservatism simply represents a rationalization for what is; what this study suggests is that Conservatism can be better understood in terms of its critique of modernity. The Conservative response to modernity deals with the political, personal, and cultural levels of man's existence.

Politically, Conservatism represents a distrust of the following political and economic trends which dominate modern society: the centralization of power and authority by national governments, the accumulation of state powers over the life of the individual, the erosion of local and community governments, the decline of rural society, the loss of community feelings and bonds, the evolution of the economy of advanced industrial societies along lines which undermine "hard property" relationships, and the growth of modern statism. In addition to opposing these trends, Conservatives also stand clearly opposed to what Voegelin terms gnostic political movements, especially the dominant form of modern gnosticism: communism.

However, the most important thing to note about the political meaning of Conservatism is that it is not the most dominant aspect of Conservative thought. Conservatives are quite distrustful of making politics the most important thing in life and would find it rather odd to see their thought defined primarily in terms of its political meaning. For instance, it is often easier to perceive the cultural meaning of Conservatism in modern society than it is to perceive its exact political meaning. In fact, many of the best Conservative critiques of modern society have their basis on the level of cultural criticism of the quality of modern life rather than being based on the level of political criticism. This is due in part to the fact that Conservative thought gives such stress to spiritual factors in its discussion of order and disorder in society. Conservatives are sometimes more concerned with questions of religion and philosophy than they are with questions about political institutions.

There is a pessimistic dimension to the Conservative's response to modernity. For its suggests that modern society is inherently disordered. Conservatives offer no escape through a great revolution that would remake society and human beings; there is no hope that the natural evolution of society will solve their most basic problems. But in speaking of Conservative pessimism over the state of modern society it is important to note that this kind of pessimism does not necessarily entail prophecies about the immediate doom of the human race, a kind of prophecy closely associated with various forms of gnostic thought that envision the destruction of everything before the emergence of a superior world. Conservative pessimism is not structured so as to be an emotional rationalization for one's own personal ideas not being triumphant in the world. It does not serve as a psychological device by which the individual damns the rest of the world and mankind for not living up to his ideals or not adopting his political theory. Rather, this pessimism is part of the tragic view of history one finds in Conservative thought.

At the present time Conservatives emphasize the spiritual and cultural tragedies they believe are entailed by modern society. Conservatives argue that modern society is inherently disordered and is an unhealthy environment for the individual. However, they require no vision of doom or eschatological ending of human existence in order to punish the world for rejecting their beliefs.

While the Conservative is deeply concerned about the state of modern society, he is not generally given to visions of immediate doom and is usually willing to try to preserve those features of his existence within the modern world he feels merit defense. Indeed, to emphasize only the pessimistic aspect of the Conservative's perception of modern society would completely overlook the truly ambivalent attitude most Conservatives have toward modernity. Despite the fact that Conservatives engage in severe critiques of the quality of modern life, they usually find enough good things about modern existence so as to argue that various aspects of modern society are worth defending. Modern industrial society has created an improved standard of living and made possible many personal freedoms that most Conservatives are anxious to defend. While contemporary Conservatives draw heavily from "traditionalist" values in their criticisms of modern society, most of them accept the "libertarian" view that the industrialization of society under democratic capitalism has been an important step forward for mankind. This in many ways represents the heart of the dilemma facing contemporary Conservatives. They desire to defend the benefits of modernity in the West, while at the same time they wish to defend the values and traditions modern society has undermined. They enjoy many of the fruits of modernity, but they complain about the price that mankind has paid.

One Conservative critic of modern society, Eric Voegelin, pays the following compliment to the accomplishments of modern, secular, scientific, rationalistic thinking:

> Gnosticism, thus, most effectively released human forces for the building of a civilization because on their fervent application to intramundane activity was put the premium of salvation. The historical result was stupendous. The resources of man that came to light under such pressure were in themselves a revelation, and their application to civilizational work produced the truly magnificent spectacle of Western progressive society. However fatuous the surface arguments may be, the widespread belief that modern civilization is Civilization in a pre-eminent sense is experientially justified; the endowment with the meaning of salvation has made the West, indeed, an apocalypse of civilization.[1]

Despite the rural perspective of many "traditionalist" Conservative thinkers, it is important to note that degree to which contemporary Conservatives have embraced the benefits of modern technology and praised the advances of the physical sciences. Indeed, in American politics today many Conservatives are enthusiastic about the space program and support nuclear energy, while a number of liberals are dubious about increasing public efforts in these areas. Also significant is the extent to which Conservatives have attacked what they call "extreme environmentalism." The Conservative response to the environmentalist movement has been much more influenced by the "libertarian" defense of industrial capitalism than the "traditionalist" idealization of rural life. Evidently many Conservatives have concluded that scientific discovery and technological innovation are essential elements of the American heritage they wish to uphold. This puts the Conservative into a paradoxical situation regarding "change."

Thus it is that contemporary Conservatives are frequently optimistic about modern society when it comes to scientific and technological progress, while often pessimistic about the decline of many traditional values. Voegelin nicely captures the spirit of those individuals who see both decline and progress in modern Western civilization:

> On the one hand, as you know, there begins in the eighteenth century a continuous stream of literature on the decline of Western civilization; and, whatever misgivings one may entertain on this or that special argument, one cannot deny that the theorists of decline on the whole have a case. On the other hand, the same period is characterized, if by anything, by an exuberantly expansive vitality in the sciences, in technology, in the material control of environment, in the increase of population, of the standard of living, of health and comfort, of mass education, of social consciousness and responsibility; and again, whatever misgivings one may entertain with regard to this or that item on the list, one cannot deny that the progressivists have a case, too. This conflict of interpretations leaves in its wake the adumbrated thorny question, that is, the question of how a civilization can advance and decline at the same time.[2]

In all of this Voegelin sees man's spiritual values being sacrificed in the pursuit of material accomplishments. The Conservative does not deny or seek to repeal the great scientific, technological, and economic gains made by modern society; however, he is likely to warn modern man that sometimes a too high price is paid for some of these material gains. Voegelin writes:

The death of the spirit is the price of progress. Nietzsche revealed this mystery of the Western apocalypse when he announced that God was dead and that He had been murdered. The Gnostic murder is constantly committed by men who sacrifice God to civilization. The more fervently all human energies are thrown into the great enterprise of salvation through world-immanent action, the farther the human beings who engage in this enterprise move away from the life of the spirit. And since the life of the spirit is the source of order in man and society, the very success of a Gnostic civilization is the cause of its decline.[3]

Just what the Conservative believes is worth defending in modern society is generally to be found in the realm of his personal existence. One cannot really understand the full meaning of Conservative thought in the context of modern society until one has dealt with its meaning on a personal level. The Conservative's Cosmological principle, his moral theory, and his theocentric humanism all have a direct bearing on the kind of life he holds the individual should try to cultivate for himself. It is much easier to see the implications that Conservatism has for the personal life of the individual than it is to see the political implications of its general principles. On a personal level Conservatism implies that the individual should try to cultivate a life based on devotion to God, family life, love, friendship, spiritual fellowship among individuals, in short, that personal conduct should be based on what was earlier termed theocentric humanism.

In a historical context in which the Conservative finds his most important religious and philosophical beliefs under increasing attacks, in a society which Conservatism views as inherently disordered, it is only natural that the meaning of Conservatism on a personal level of existence would become highlighted. That an individual should try to order his life along Conservative lines in the non-Conservative context of modern society is no easy task. Indeed, Conservative thought suggests that it is particularly difficult to do so. But it is here on the level of the individual's personal existence where Conservatism finds its greatest meaning in modern society, for it is here where the Conservative believes that the struggle for the individual's soul takes place, where the stakes are the greatest. Conservatism does not promise an idyllic existence to an individual who tries to order his life along these lines, especially in modern society. However, it is in regard to the personal life and development of the individual that the Conservative speaks with the greatest concern and clarity.

The final meaning of Conservatism within the context of modern society is to be found on the cultural level. The Conservative's concern for the personal life of the individual leads immediately to his concern for the quality of modern life and culture. Much of Conservative thought for the last three hundred years can be understood as a continuing cultural protest against the differing life styles adopted by modern man. In this connection one need only think of the works of T. S. Eliot or Ortega y Gasset. Cultural protest against the quality of modern life is a constant theme to be found in Conservative thought; it often overshadows what Conservatives have had to say about political and economic issues. One may even say that as long as modern society is fashioned by the values now so predominant, the meaning of Conservatism on a cultural level will remain one of the crucial aspects of the Conservative's thinking and will serve him as a continuing basis for social criticism. What Conservatism says about cultural life can hardly be separated from its view of the kind of life it believes the individual should try to cultivate. The personal and cultural meanings of Conservative thought in the context of modern society are closely bound together and constitute the heart of Conservatism.

The great problem facing Conservative thought in the twentieth century concerns how the Conservative plans to protect the values associated with his vision of man's personal existence and the values associated with his view of culture from those of society at large and the state. Here one encounters the weakest point of Conservative thought. It is only reasonable to expect of a political theory that it offer a clear idea of how to protect or advance its most important values: in the case of Conservative political thought, to protect its most important values from the impact of current political decisions and from developments taking place in society at large. In the context of modern society it is difficult to distinguish what is public and private, nonpolitical and political, and just as difficult to find areas of personal existence not affected by politics.

The response of so many Conservatives to the problem has generally been to argue against the growth of the powers and responsibilities of the nation state and to try to seal off certain aspects of the individual's life from control and regulation by the state. This response, of course, represents the point where Conservatism shares so much in common with classical liberalism. Here one understands the political meaning of Conservatism in terms of what it opposes: the erosion of property rights, the growth of the public sector of the economy at the expense of the private sector, and the always expanding governmental regulation of the individual's life. Thus the Reagan administration tries to reduce taxes, slow the growth of federal spending, reduce government regulation of business, and decentralize political authority in the American federal system of government. Such proposals serve many important Conservative objectives.

However, such proposals do not constitute an adequate response to many of the larger dangers threatening Conservative values in modern society.

Even if Conservatives were to be successful in their struggle against the political and economic trends which dominate modern society (and it is difficult to see how they could be successful in reversing all these trends), one could still doubt whether that victory would translate into adequate protection of their most important cultural and personal values. The political position of most contemporary Conservatives, while providing some means of protecting certain Conservative values from flagrant violation, hardly serves as a means of protecting other values from the underlying developments associated with the advance of modern society. Imagine the unlikely, that Conservatives were successful in halting the growth of the powers and responsibilities of the nation state over the life of the individual, the erosion of community and local governments, and the growth of Communism and the spread of revolutionary political movements. Even if Conservatives were politically victorious along these lines, one can seriously doubt whether such a victory would protect other important values from the other underlying social and philosophical developments associated with the advance of modernity. Conservative political theory offers no real way to deal with these phenomena and the dangers they pose to basic Conservative values.

Here one can see the danger of a real breakdown in the relationship between theoretical and practical reason in Conservative political thinking. While the Conservative can succeed in at least suggesting how to defend certain political values and goals, he offers no way to deal successfully with the dangers threatening his most important personal and cultural values. Part of this problem may be traced to the inherent weakness of the position many Conservatives share with classical liberals, the position which conceptualizes the solution to the basic problems facing modern man in terms of reducing the role of the nation state in regulating the life of the individual. Certainly one may think of many Conservative values and political principles which have been endangered by the growth of modern nation states. This helps to explain the quite justifiable attraction many Conservatives feel toward political and economic aspects of classical liberalism. But crucial dangers to basic Conservative values also come from beyond the direct reach of state activities; many dangers come from developments within society at large and are outside the scope of the classical liberal view of how to protect basic values. The problem here is not so much that the political position of so many Conservatives has been "wrong," for one can see how that position does protect many important Conservative values, but that the position has simply been inadequate for protecting many other important values. Even if modern society were to convert to an essentially laissez-faire economic system, this would, by itself, do nothing to guarantee that the life of the individual or the cultural life of the nation would be structured according to the values of theocentric humanism, for example.

What plagues modern man, for the Conservative, is the alienation of man from traditional religion, moral values, and social bonds. As Robert Nisbet writes:

> The modern release of the individual from traditional ties of class, religion, and kinship has made him free; but, not on the testimony of innumerable works in our age, this freedom is accompanied not only by the sense of creative release but by the sense of disenchantment and alienation. The alienation of man from historic moral certitude has been followed by the sense of man's alienation from fellow man.[4]

According to Nisbet modern man is increasingly cut off from the social order:

> By alienation I mean the state of mind that can find a social order remote, incomprehensible, or fraudulent; beyond real hope or desire; inviting apathy, boredom, or even hostility. The individual not only does not feel a part of the social order; he has lost interest in being a part of it.[5]

According to the Conservative interpretation of alienation, modernity continually makes war against what each man and society need for a meaningful existence—the past. Nisbet writes:

> There is, first, alienation from the past. Man, it is said, is a time-binding creature; past and future are as important to his natural sense of identity as the present. Destroy his sense of the past, and you cut his spiritual roots, leaving momentary febrility but no viable prospect of the future.

In our age, as we are frequently told, past and present are not merely separated categories but discontinuous ones in the lives of large numbers of persons, more than a few of whom have consciously sought escape from their past.[6]

The ignorance of history which Conservatives have observed in recent generations has coincided with the reduction of history requirements at major colleges and universities in the United States during the last three decades. For the Conservative, people without a fundamental conception of their past are people who have no guide for their future.

That Conservative political theory has thus far shown itself to be insufficient for dealing with the dangers that modernity poses to its basic values does not mean that it is of no value and has nothing of importance to say to modern man. Conservative thought, through its theocentric humanism, which is premodern in its basic orientation, has very much to say to modern man. Modernity, patterned on a very different way of perceiving man and his place in the universe, has certainly released vital creative energies that have transformed man's material existence. The Conservative can hardly overlook the technical and scientific accomplishments of the modern era. Modern society has indeed created unparalleled opportunities for the individual and freed man from many of the horrors once confronting the existence of the individual. Nevertheless, the Conservative argues that the spiritual cost of modernity has been great. On this score the Conservative is able to address himself to the uneasy conscience of modern man and to the loneliness of the individual in modern society. Modernity has brought with it considerable unhappiness; there is, for so many people, a great feeling of emptiness and spiritual darkness. Here, Conservatism, through its theocentric humanism, offers the individual a way of thinking about his own existence and place in the universe that expands the relatively more narrow horizons one encounters in modern thought. Through its personal and cultural values Conservatism offers modern man an opportunity to discover a new mode of living which might make possible a greater sense of meaning for the life of the individual.

The challenge to Conservative thought in all this is as great as its opportunity. Many basic Conservative values have a great attraction to people in modern society who find contemporary values and culture to be relatively meaningless. It is not extremely difficult to make the Conservative vision of what man's personal existence should be like sound attractive to men who live in a society suffering from the consequences of the decline in traditional religious values, family bonds, and community relationships. But if Conservative thought is to take advantage of the opportunities presented to it because of the potential attractiveness of many of its basic values, it must somehow devise a political theory that really addresses itself to the problem of how to deal with the substantial threats that modernity poses to its most important values.

Notes

1. The Religious Orientation of Conservatism

1. Robert Nisbet, "A Note on Conservatism," in *The Works of Joseph de Maistre*, ed. Jack Lively (New York: Schocken Books, 1971), p. xiv. Reprinted by permission. Copyright © 1965 by Jack Lively. Introduction copyright © 1971 by Robert Nisbet.

2. Clinton Rossiter, *Conservatism in America: The Thankless Persuasion*, 2nd ed., rev. (New York: Alfred A. Knopf, 1964), p. 42.

3. Jacques Maritain, *True Humanism* (London: Geoffrey Bles: The Centenary Press, 1938), p. 19.

4. Dante Germino, *Modern Western Political Thought: Machiavelli to Marx* (Chicago: Rand McNally and Company, 1972), p. 15.

5. Edmund Burke, *Reflections on the Revolution in France* (New York: Holt, Rinehart and Winston, 1959, 1962), p. 110.

6. Ibid., p. 109.

7. Eric Voegelin, *The New Science of Politics* (Chicago: University of Chicago Press, 1952), chapters 4, 5, 6.

8. Burke, *Reflections on the Revolution in France*, p. 11.

9. Karl Mannheim, *Ideology and Utopia* (New York: Harcourt, Brace and World, 1936), pp. 11–12.

10. Karl Mannheim, *From Karl Mannheim* (New York: Oxford University Press, 1971), pp. 143–144.

2. The Conservative View of Human Nature

1. Edmund Burke, *The Works and Correspondence of Ed-*

mund Burke, vol. 6 (London: Gilber and Rivington Printers, 1852), p. 132.

2. Peter Stanlis, *Edmund Burke and the Natural Law* (Ann Arbor: University of Michigan Press, 1958), p. 127.

3. R. J. White, *The Conservative Tradition* (London: A. and C. Black Limited, 1950), p. 4.

4. Edmund Burke, *Reflections on the Revolution in France* (New York: Holt, Rinehart and Winston, 1959, 1962), pp. 227–228.

5. Alan Ryan, "The Nature of Human Nature in Hobbes and Rousseau," in *The Limits of Human Nature*, ed. Jonathan Benthall (New York: E. P. Dutton and Company, 1974), p. 13.

6. C. S. Lewis, *Mere Christianity* (New York: Macmillan Company, 1943, 1945, 1952), pp. 31–32.

7. Burleigh T. Wilkins, *The Problem of Burke's Political Philosophy* (Oxford: Oxford University Press, 1967), p. 91.

3. The Conservative View of Human Reason

1. Edmund Burke, "Appeal from the New to the Old Whigs," in *The Philosophy of Edmund Burke*, ed. Louis Bredvold and Ralph Ross (Ann Arbor: University of Michigan Press, 1960), p. 41.

2. Michael Oakeshott, *Rationalism in Politics* (London: Methuen, 1962), p. 11.

3. Edmund Burke, *The Works and Correspondence of Edmund Burke*, vol. 6 (London: Gilber and Rivington Printers, 1852), p. 101.

4. Edmund Burke, *Reflections on the Revolution in France* (New York: Holt, Rinehart and Winston, 1959, 1962), p. 6.

5. Francis P. Canavan, *The Political Reason of Edmund Burke* (Durham, N.C.: Duke University Press, 1960), p. 8.

6. Karl Mannheim, *From Karl Mannheim* (New York: Oxford University Press, 1971), pp. 160–161.

7. Francis P. Canavan, *The Political Reason of Edmund Burke*, p. 50.

8. Leo Strauss, *Natural Right and History* (Chicago: University of Chicago Press, 1953), pp. 302–303.

9. Edmund Burke, *Reflections on the Revolution in France*, p. 105.

10. Dante Germino, *Modern Western Political Thought: Machiavelli to Marx* (Chicago: Rand McNally and Company, 1972), p. 225.

11. Ibid., p. 215.

12. Francis P. Canavan, *The Political Reason of Edmund Burke*, p. 75.

13. Leon Bramson, *The Political Context of Sociology* (Princeton, N.J.: Princeton University Press, 1961), p. 16.

14. Klaus Epstein, *The Genesis of German Conservatism* (Princeton, New Jersey: Princeton University Press, 1966), p. 14.

15. Immanuel Kant, "What Is Enlightenment?" in *The Liberal Tradition in European Thought*, ed. David Sidorsky (New York: G. P. Putnam's Sons, 1970), p. 65.

16. C. S. Lewis, *Mere Christianity* (New York: Macmillan Company, 1943, 1945, 1952), pp. 63–64.

17. C. S. Lewis, *The Abolition of Man* (New York: Macmillan Company, 1947), pp. 33–34.

18. Edmund Burke, "Speech on the Unitarians," in *The Works and Correspondence of Edmund Burke*, vol. 6, p. 101.

19. Edmund Burke, "Speech on Reform of Representation," in *The Works and Correspondence of Edmund Burke*, vol. 6, pp. 131–132.

20. Francis P. Canavan, "Edmund Burke's Conception of the Role of Reason in Politics," *The Journal of Politics*, vol. 21, no. 1 (December 1959): 75–76.

4. The Moral Theory and Value System of Conservatism

1. Edmund Burke, *The Philosophy of Edmund Burke*, ed. Louis Bredvold and Ralph Ross (Ann Arbor: University of Michigan Press, 1960), p. 17.

2. Edmund Burke, "An Appeal from the New to the Old Whigs," in *The Works and Correspondence of Edmund Burke*, vol. 4 (London: Gilber and Rivington Printers, 1852), p. 460.

3. Ibid., pp. 460–461.

4. Francis P. Canavan, *The Political Reason of Edmund Burke* (Durham, N.C.: Duke University Press, 1960), p. 126.

5. Leo Strauss, *Natural Right and History* (Chicago: University of Chicago Press, 1953), p. 3.

6. Ibid., p. 13.

7. Edmund Burke, *Reflections on the Revolution in France* (New York: Holt, Rinehart and Winston, 1959, 1962), p. 74.

8. Ibid., p. 73.

9. Eric Voegelin, *Plato and Aristotle*, vol. 3, *Order and History* (Baton Rouge: Louisiana State University Press, 1957), p. 112.

10. Leo Strauss, *Natural Right and History*, p. 6.

11. Ibid., p. 5.

12. C. S. Lewis, *The Abolition of Man* (London: Oxford University Press, 1944), pp. 41–48.

13. Edmund Burke, *Reflections on the Revolution in France*, p. 304.

14. Edmund Burke, "Speech at His Arrival to Bristol," in *The Works and Correspondence of Edmund Burke*, vol. 3, p. 230.

15. Edmund Burke, *Reflections on the Revolution in France*, p. 6.

16. Russell Kirk, "Prescription, Authority, and Ordered Freedom," in *What Is Conservatism?*, ed. Frank Meyer (New York: Holt, Rinehart and Winston, 1964), p. 24.

17. Burleigh T. Wilkins, *The Problem of Burke's Political Philosophy* (Oxford: Oxford University Press, 1967), p. 249.

18. Frank Meyer, "Freedom, Tradition, Conservatism," in *What Is Conservatism?*, p. 8.

19. Ibid., pp. 13–14.

20. Ibid., p. 16.

21. Ibid., p. 14.

22. Ibid., p. 16.

5. Conservatism and the Foundations of Order

1. Edmund Burke, *Reflections on the Revolution in France* (New York: Holt, Rinehart and Winston, 1959, 1962), p. 117.

2. T. S. Eliot, *Notes towards the Definition of Culture* (New York: Harcourt, Brace and Company, 1949), pp. 16–17.

3. Ibid., p. 13.

4. Stanley Parry, "Reason and the Restoration of Tradition," in *What Is Conservatism?*, ed. Frank Meyer (New York: Holt, Rinehart, and Winston, 1964), pp. 115–116.

5. T. S. Eliot, *The Idea of a Christian Society* (New York: Harcourt, Brace and Company, 1940), p. 13.

6. Stanley Parry, "Reason and the Restoration of Tradition," pp. 109–110.

7. Edmund Burke, *Reflections on the Revolution in France,* pp. 103–104.

8. Frank Meyer, "Freedom, Tradition, Conservatism," in *What Is Conservatism?*, ed. Frank Meyer, p. 13.

9. Willmoore Kendall and George Carey, "Towards a Definition of Conservatism," *The Journal of Politics*, vol. 26, no. 2 (May 1964): 410.

10. Frank Meyer, "Freedom, Tradition, Conservatism," in *What Is Conservatism?*, ed. Frank Meyer, p. 10.

11. Morton Auerbach, *The Conservative Illusion* (New York: Columbia University Press, 1959), p. 18.

12. T. S. Eliot, *Notes towards the Definition of Culture*, pp. 17–18.

13. Quintin Hogg, *The Case for Conservatism* (London: Penguin Books, 1947), p. 10.

14. Edmund Burke, "An Appeal from the New to the Old Whigs," in *The Works and Correspondence of Edmund Burke*, vol. 4 (London: Gilber and Rivington Printers, 1852), p. 407.

15. Edmund Burke, *Reflections on the Revolution in France*, p. 210.

16. Ibid., p. 77.

17. Thucydides, *The Peloponnesian War*, ed. John Finley, Jr. (New York: Random House, 1951), p. 189.

18. Edmund Burke, "An Appeal from the New to the Old Whigs," p. 407.

19. Edmund Burke, *Reflections on the Revolution in France*, p. 23.

20. Klaus Epstein, *The Genesis of German Conservatism* (Princeton: Princeton University Press, 1966), p. 18.

21. R. J. White, *The Conservative Tradition* (London: A. and C. Black Limited, 1950), p. 3.

22. Edmund Burke, *Reflections on the Revolution in France*, p. 193.

23. T. S. Eliot, *Notes towards the Definitions of Culture*, p. 85.

24. John Adams, *The Works of John Adams*, ed. C. F. Adams, vol. 10 (Boston: Charles C. Little and James Brown, 1850–1856), p. 174.

25. Edmund Burke, *Reflections on the Revolution in France*, p. 153.

26. Klaus Epstein, *The Genesis of German Conservatism*, p. 313.

27. James Madison, "Federalist Paper No. 10," in *The Federalist Papers* (New York: The New American Library, 1961), p. 322.

28. Alexis de Tocqueville, *Democracy in America*, vol. 1 (New Rochelle, N.Y.: Arlington House, 1966), p. 77.

29. Edmund Burke, *Reflections on the Revolution in France*, p. 55.

30. T. S. Eliot, *Notes towards the Definition of Culture*, p. 51.

31. Clinton Rossiter, *Conservatism in America: The Thankless Persuasion*, 2nd ed., rev. (New York: Alfred A. Knopf, 1964), p. 38.

32. Edmund Burke, *Reflections on the Revolution in France*, pp. 60–61.

33. Karl Mannheim, *From Karl Mannheim*, ed. Kurt Wolff (New York: Oxford University Press, 1971), p. 162.

34. Ibid., p. 163.

35. John C. Calhoun, *A Disquisition on Government* (Indianapolis: Bobbs-Merrill Company, 1953), p. 44.

36. Ibid., pp. 43–44.

37. James Madison, "Federalist Paper No. 10," pp. 78–79.

6. The Relationship between Theoretical and Practical Reason in Conservative Thought

1. C. E. Lindblom, "The Handling of Norms in Policy Analysis," in *Allocation of Economic Resources*, ed. M. Ambramovitz (Stanford: Stanford University Press, 1958), p. 163.

2. C. E. Lindblom, "Tinbergen on Policy Making," *Journal of Political Economy* 66 (1958): 535.

3. Edmund Burke, *Reflections on the Revolution in France*

(New York: Holt, Rinehart and Winston, 1959, 1962), p. 126.

4. Thomas Aquinas, *The Political Ideas of St. Thomas Aquinas*, ed. Dino Bigongiari (New York: Hafner Publishing Company, 1953), p. 68.

5. Clinton Rossiter, *Conservatism in America: The Thankless Persuasion*, 2nd ed., rev. (New York: Alfred A. Knopf, 1964), p. 44.

6. Stanley Parry, "Reason and the Restoration of Tradition," in *What Is Conservatism?*, ed. Frank S. Meyer (New York: Holt, Rinehart and Winston, 1964), p. 108.

7. Edmund Burke, *Reflections on the Revolution in France*, pp. 105–106.

Conclusion

1. Eric Voegelin, *The New Science of Politics* (Chicago: University of Chicago Press, 1952), p. 130.

2. Ibid., pp. 128–129.

3. Ibid., p. 131.

4. Robert A. Nisbet, *The Quest for Community* (New York: Oxford University Press, 1953), p. 10.

5. Ibid., p. ix.

6. Ibid., p. x.

Bibliography

John Adams. *The Works of John Adams.* Edited by C. F. Adams. 10 vols. Boston: Charles C. Little and James Brown, 1850–1856.

Thomas Aquinas. *The Political Ideas of St. Thomas Aquinas.* Edited by Dino Bigongiari. New York: Hafner Publishing Company, 1969.

Hannah Arendt. *The Human Condition.* Chicago: University of Chicago Press, 1958.

Raymond Aron. *Main Currents in Sociological Thought.* Vol. 1. Garden City, New York: Doubleday & Company, 1968.

Morton Auerbach. *The Conservative Illusion.* New York: Columbia University Press, 1959.

Leon Bramson. *The Political Context of Sociology.* Princeton, New Jersey: Princeton University Press, 1961.

William F. Buckley, Jr. "The Failure of the Conservative Demonstration." In *The Wisdom of Conservatism*, edited by Peter Witonski, vol. 4. New Rochelle, New York: Arlington House, 1971. This selection is taken from Buckley's *Up from Liberalism*.

Edmund Burke. *The Correspondence of Edmund Burke.* Edited by Thomas W. Copeland. 10 vols. Cambridge: Cambridge University Press; Chicago: Chicago University Press, 1958.

Edmund Burke. *The Philosophy of Edmund Burke.* Edited by Louis Bredvold and Ralph Ross. Ann Arbor: University of Michigan Press, 1960.

Edmund Burke. *Reflections on the Revolution in France.* New York: Holt, Rinehart and Winston, 1959, 1962.

Edmund Burke. *The Works and Correspondence of Edmund Burke.* 8 vols. London: Gilber and Rivington Printers, 1852.

John C. Calhoun. *A Disquisition on Government.* Indianapolis: Bobbs-Merrill Company, 1953.

Francis P. Canavan. *The Political Reason of Edmund Burke.* Durham, North Carolina: Duke University Press, 1960.

Francis P. Canavan. "Edmund Burke's Conception of the Role of Reason in Politics." *The Journal of Politics,* vol. 21, no. 1 (February 1959): 60–79.

Alfred Cobban. *Edmund Burke and the Revolt against the Eighteenth Century.* 2nd ed. (first was in 1929). London: Allen & Unwin, 1960.

Carl B. Cone. *Burke and the Nature of Politics.* 2 vols. Lexington, Kentucky: University of Kentucky Press, 1957.

Seymour Drescher. *Dilemmas of Democracy: Tocqueville and Modernization.* Pittsburg: University of Pittsburg Press, 1968.

T. S. Eliot. *The Idea of a Christian Society.* New York: Harcourt, Brace and Company, 1940.

T. S. Eliot. *Notes towards the Definition of Culture.* New York: Harcourt, Brace and Company, 1949.

Klaus Epstein. *The Genesis of German Conservatism.* Princeton, New Jersey: Princeton University Press, 1966.

Edward T. Gargan. *Alexis de Tocqueville: The Critical Years 1848–1851.* Washington, D.C.: Catholic University of America Press, 1955.

Dante Germino. "Burke and the Reaction against the French Revolution." In *Modern Western Political Thought: Machiavelli to Marx.* Chicago: Rand McNally and Company, 1972.

Doris S. Goldstein, "The Religious Beliefs of Alex de Tocqueville." *French Historical Studies,* vol. 1, no. 4 (Dec. 1960): 379–394.

Allen Guttmann. *The Conservative Tradition in America.* New York: Oxford University Press, 1967.

Alexander Hamilton, John Jay, and James Madison. *The Federalist Papers.* New York: New American Library, 1961.

Quinton Hogg. *The Case for Conservatism.* London: Penguin Books, 1947.

Willmoore Kendall and George W. Carey. *The Basic Symbols of the American Political Tradition.* Baton Rouge: Louisiana State University Press, 1970.

Willmoore Kendall and George W. Carey. "Towards a Definition of Conservatism." *The Journal of Politics*, vol. 26, no. 2 (May 1964) : 406–22.

Russell Kirk. *The Conservative Mind from Burke to Santayana.* Chicago: Henry Regnery, 1953.

Klemens von Klemperer. *Germany's New Conservatism: Its History and Dilemma in the Twentieth Century.* Princeton, New Jersey: Princeton University Press, 1957, 1968.

C. S. Lewis. *The Abolition of Man.* London: Oxford University Press, 1944; New York: Macmillan Company, 1947.

C. S. Lewis. *Mere Christianity.* New York: Macmillan Company, 1943, 1945, 1952.

C. E. Lindblom. "The Handling of Norms in Policy Analysis." In *Allocation of Economic Resources*, edited by M. Ambramovitz. Stanford: Stanford University Press, 1958.

C. E. Lindblom. "Tinbergen on Policy Making." *Journal of Political Economy*, no. 66 (Dec. 1958) : 531–538.

Jack Lively. *The Social and Political Thought of Alexis de Tocqueville.* London: Oxford University Press, Clarendon Press, 1962.

Joseph de Maistre. *The Works of Joseph de Maistre.* Edited by Jack Lively, with a foreword by Robert Nisbet (1971) entitled "A Note on Conservatism." New York: Schocken Books, 1965.

Karl Mannheim. *From Karl Mannheim.* Edited and with an introduction by Kurt H. Wolff. New York: Oxford University Press, 1971.

Karl Mannheim. *Ideology and Utopia.* New York: Harcourt, Brace and World, 1936.

Jacques Maritain. *True Humanism.* London: Geoffrey Bles: The Centenary Press, 1938.

Frank S. Meyer, ed. *What Is Conservatism?* New York: Holt, Rinehart and Winston, 1964.

Thomas Molnar. *The Counter-Revolution.* New York: Funk and Wagnalls, 1969.

Thomas Molnar. *Utopia, The Perennial Heresy.* New York: Sheed and Ward, 1967.

George H. Nash. *The Conservative Intellectual Movement in America Since 1945.* New York: Basic Books, 1976.

John Henry Newman, "Appendix on Liberalism." In *The Wis-*

dom of Conservatism, edited by Peter Witonski, vol. 1. New Rochelle, New York: Arlington House, 1971. This selection is from Newman's *Apologia Pro Vita Sua*.

Robert A. Nisbet. *The Sociological Tradition*. New York: Basic Books, 1966.

Robert A. Nisbet. *The Quest for Community*. New York: Oxford University Press, 1953.

Michael Oakeshott. *Rationalism in Politics*. London: Methuen, 1962.

Stanley Parry. "Reason and the Restoration of Tradition." In *What Is Conservatism?*, edited by Frank S. Meyer. New York: Holt, Rinehart and Winston, 1964.

Hanna Pitkin. "The Roots of Conservatism: Michael Oakeshott and the Denial of Politics." *Dissent*, fall 1973, pp. 496–525.

Clinton Rossiter. *Conservatism in America: The Thankless Persuasion*. 2nd ed., rev. New York: Alfred A. Knopf, 1964. Original edition 1955.

Alan Ryan. "The Nature of Human Nature in Hobbes and Rousseau." In *The Limits of Human Nature*, edited by Jonathan Benthall. New York: E. P. Dutton and Company, 1974.

Robert Schuettinger, ed. *The Conservative Tradition in European Thought*. New York: G. P. Putnam's Sons, 1970.

David Sidorsky, ed. *The Liberal Tradition in European Thought*. New York: G. P. Putnam's Sons, 1970.

Peter J. Stanlis. *Edmund Burke and the Natural Law*. Ann Arbor: University of Michigan Press, 1958.

Richard Stellway. "The Correspondence between Religious Orientation and Socio-Political Liberalism and Conservatism." *Sociological Quarterly* 14 (summer, 1973) : 430–439.

Fritz Stern. *The Politics of Cultural Despair*. Berkeley: University of California Press, 1961.

Leo Strauss. *Natural Right and History*. Chicago: University of Chicago Press, 1953.

Thucydides. *The Peloponnesian War*. Introduction by John H. Finley, Jr. New York: Random House, 1951.

Alexis de Tocqueville. *Correspondence and Conversations of Alexis de Tocqueville with Nassau William Senior*. Edited by M. C. M. Simpson. 2 vols. London: Henry S. King and Company, 1872.

Alexis de Tocqueville. *Democracy in America*. Translated by

Henry Reeve, introduction by Erik von Kuehnelt-Leddihn. Vol. 1. New Rochelle, New York: Arlington House, 1966.

Alexis de Tocqueville. *Democracy in America.* Translated by Henry Reeve. Vol. 2. New York: Alfred A. Knopf, 1963.

Alexis de Tocqueville. *The European Revolution and Correspondence with Gobineau.* Edited by John Lukacs. Gloucester, Mass.: Peter Smith, 1968.

Alexis de Tocqueville. *Journeys to England and Ireland.* Translated by George Lawrence and K. P. Mayer, edited by J. P. Mayer. New Haven: Yale University Press, 1958.

Alexis de Tocqueville. *The Old Regime and the French Revolution.* Translated by Stuart Gilbert. Garden City, New York: Doubleday/Anchor Books, 1955.

Alexis de Tocqueville. *The Recollections of Alexis de Tocqueville.* Edited by J. P. Mayer. Morningside Heights, New York: Columbia University Press, 1949.

Peter Viereck. *Conservatism from John Adams to Churchill.* New York: D. Van Nostrand Company, 1956.

Peter Viereck. *Conservatism Revisited.* Revised and enlarged edition with the addition of Book II: The New Conservatism: What Went Wrong? New York: Free Press, 1949, 1962.

Eliseo Vivas. *Contra Marcuse.* New Rochelle, New York: Arlington House, 1971.

Eric Voegelin. *The New Science of Politics.* Chicago: University of Chicago Press, 1952.

Eric Voegelin. "On Classical Studies." *Modern Age*, vol. 17, no. 1 (winter, 1973): 3–8.

Eric Voegelin. "On Debate and Existence." *The Intercollegiate Review*, vol. 3, nos. 4–5 (March-April, 1967): 143–152.

Eric Voegelin. *Order and History.* 4 vols. Baton Rouge: Louisiana State University Press, 1956, 1957, 1957, 1975.

Richard M. Weaver. *The Ethics of Rhetoric.* Chicago: Henry Regnery Company, 1953.

Richard M. Weaver. *Ideas Have Consequences.* Chicago: University of Chicago Press, 1948.

Richard M. Weaver. *Life without Prejudice and Other Essays.* Introduction by Eliseo Vivas. Chicago: Henry Regnery Company, 1965.

Richard M. Weaver. *Visions of Order: The Cultural Crisis of Our Time.* Baton Rouge: Louisiana State University Press, 1964.

R. J. White. *The Anti-Philosophers: A Study of the Philosophes in Eighteenth-Century France.* London: Macmillan and Company, 1970.

R. J. White. *The Conservative Tradition.* London: A. and C. Black Limited, 1950.

Burleigh Taylor Wilkins. *The Problem of Burke's Political Philosophy.* Oxford: Oxford University Press, Clarendon Press, 1967.

Francis Graham Wilson. *The Case for Conservatism.* Seattle: University of Washington Press, 1951.

Peter Witonski, ed. *The Wisdom of Conservatism.* 4 vols. New Rochelle, New York: Arlington House, 1971.

Irving Zeitlin. *Liberty, Equality, and Revolution in Alexis de Tocqueville.* Boston: Little, Brown and Company, 1971.

Marvin Zetterbaum. *Tocqueville and the Problem of Democracy.* Stanford: Stanford University Press, 1967.

Biographical List

JOHN ADAMS. 1735–1826. Second president of the United States (1797–1801). His views on human nature, the need for government, the causes of political conflict, and theory of the mixed constitution are of considerable importance to American Conservatism. Author of *A Defence of the Constitutions of Government of the United States of America* (3 volumes, 1787–1788).

SAINT THOMAS AQUINAS. 1225?–1274. Most influential Catholic philosopher of the Middle Ages. This Italian Scholastic thinker's attempt to develop a synthesis of Aristotelian philosophy and Christian thought captures the aspirations of those Conservatives who wish to defend both the Greek and Christian traditions as essential to Western civilization. Author of *Summa Theologica*.

ARISTOTLE. 384–322 B.C. Famous Greek philosopher. His method of thought, view of man as a social being, analysis of the causes of revolution, support for a middle-class polity, and emphasis on the development of a stable society are important to Conservative thought. Author of the *Politics*.

MORTON AUERBACH. 1924– . A critic of Conservative thought. Author of *The Conservative Illusion* (1959).

WALTER BERNS. 1919– . American political theorist. An influential defender of traditional Conservative values. Author of *Freedom, Virtue and the First Amendment* (1957).

LEON BRAMSON. 1930– . American sociologist. Author of *The Political Context of Sociology* (1961).

EDMUND BURKE. 1729–1797. British statesman and orator, generally viewed as the father of modern Conservatism. His critique of the French Revolution stands as a classic piece of Conservative thinking. Author of *Reflections on the Revolution in France* (1790).

JOHN C. CALHOUN. 1782–1850. Seventh vice-president of the United States (1825–1832). This Southern statesman's ideas on human nature, the abuses of political power, and theory of the "concurrent majority" are an important part of American Conservatism. Author of *A Disquisition on Government* (1853).

FRANCIS P. CANAVAN. 1917–   . American political and religious thinker. Author of *The Political Reason of Edmund Burke* (1960).

GEORGE W. CAREY. 1926–   . American political scientist. An authority on the political thought of the founding fathers. Author, along with Willmoore Kendall, of *The Basic Symbols of the American Political Tradition* (1970).

JAMES EARL CARTER, JR. 1924–   . Thirty-ninth president of the United States (1977–1981).

LORD HUGH CECIL. 1869–1956. British statesman and author of *Conservatism* (1912).

SAMUEL TAYLOR COLERIDGE. 1772–1834. British poet and philosopher. While a radical in his youth, his later works have had considerable impact on traditionalist Conservative thinking. Besides such famous poems as "The Rime of the Ancient Mariner" he is also the author of *Biographia Literaria* (1817) and *Church and State* (1830).

RENÉ DESCARTES. 1596–1650. French philosopher and mathematician generally viewed as one of the originators of modern philosophy. His rationalist system of thought and desire for mathematical certitude are criticized by most Conservatives. Author of the essay *Discourse on Method* (1637).

BENJAMIN DISRAELI. 1804–1881. Prime minister of Great Britain (1868, 1874–1880). Influential Conservative critic of nineteenth-century liberalism. He is often cited as an example by those Conservatives who wish to support the welfare state. Author of *Coningsby* (1844) and *Sybil* (1845).

T. S. ELIOT. 1888–1965. American-born British poet, literary critic, and dramatist. His powerful poems and dramas capture much of the Conservative critique of modern culture and society. Author of the poem *The Waste Land* (1922) and prose works *The Idea of a Christian Society* (1940) and *Notes Towards a Definition of Culture* (1948).

KLAUS EPSTEIN. 1927– . An authority on German political thinking. Author of *The Genesis of German Conservatism* (1966).

MILTON FRIEDMAN. 1912– . Economist. Leading monetary theorist, defender of capitalism, and advocate of laissez-faire liberalism in the United States. His ideas about a free-market economy exercise great influence on contemporary Conservatives. Author of *A Monetary History of the United States, 1867–1960* (1963) and *Capitalism and Freedom* (1962).

DANTE GERMINO. – . American political theorist. A defender of theocentric humanism. Author of *Modern Western Political Thought: Machiavelli to Marx* (1972).

GEORGE GILDER. 1939– . American political theorist. Defender of supply-side economics. Author of *Wealth and Poverty* (1981).

ALEXANDER HAMILTON. 1755–1804. American statesman and first secretary of the Treasury (1789–1795). His arguments for strong government and interventionist economic policies represent that wing of Conservative thought which does not feel at home with laissez-faire liberalism. Along with Madison and Jay he was an author of *The Federalist Papers* (1787–1788).

WARREN HASTINGS. 1732–1818. British administrator in India whose impeachment was sought by Edmund Burke.

FRIEDRICH A. HAYEK. 1899– . Austrian-born economist. A leading defender of free-market economics and the Whig tradition of political thought. Author of *The Road to Serfdom* (1944) and *The Constitution of Liberty* (1960).

GEORG WILHELM FRIEDRICH HEGEL. 1770–1831. German philosopher. His philosophy of history, dialectical method, and ideas about the state show up in nineteenth- and twentieth-century political thinking both on the far left and far right of the political spectrum. Author of *The Philosophy of Right* (1821).

CLAUDE ADRIEN HELVETIUS. 1715–1771. French philosopher. Noted materialist and author of *De l'esprit* (1758).

THOMAS HOBBES. 1588–1679. English philosopher. Sometimes viewed as one of the originators of modern political philosophy. His account of the shortcomings of human nature and plea for strong government continue to have impact on modern political thought. He is one of the greatest expounders of the social contract theory of government. Author of the *Leviathan* (1651).

QUINTIN HOGG. 1907–   . British statesman and political thinker. Author of *The Case for Conservatism* (1947).

THOMAS JEFFERSON. 1743–1826. Third president of the United States (1801–1809). This American statesman and political thinker is usually associated with liberal political thought. However, Conservatives admire his arguments for limited constitutional government and individual freedom. Principal author of *The Declaration of Independence* (1776).

LYNDON BAINES JOHNSON. 1908–1973. Thirty-sixth president of the United States (1963–1969). Much of contemporary Conservative political thought represents a critique of his Great Society programs.

IMMANUEL KANT. 1724–1804. German philosopher. His analysis of human knowledge, examination of the basis of ethical ideas, belief in the autonomy of each person, and argument that freedom must be understood in terms of being subject to laws that reason leads man to give to himself make him one of the most influential thinkers of modern times. Author of *Critique of Pure Reason* (1781) and *Metaphysics of Morals* (1797).

WILLMOORE KENDALL. 1909–1967. American political theorist. His study of the problems of majority rule and analysis of federalism have had considerable impact on Conservative thought. Author of *John Locke and the Doctrine of Majority Rule* (1941).

RUSSELL KIRK. 1918–   . American political thinker and author of dozens of books and articles advancing traditionalist Conservative values. One of the most important Conservative thinkers of this century. Author of *The Conservative Mind* (1953).

IRVING KRISTOL. 1922–   . One of the leading neo-Conservatives in America today. Coeditor of the journal *The Public Interest* and influential columnist. He has taken the lead among those former liberals who have rejected Great Society liberalism in very Conservative terms. Author of *Two Cheers for Capitalism* (1978).

C. S. LEWIS. 1898–1963. British novelist and critic. His defense of Christianity and traditional moral values makes him quite popular among Conservatives. Author of *Mere Christianity* (1943) and *The Abolition of Man* (1944).

CHARLES E. LINDBLOM. 1917– . American political and economic theorist. Author, along with Robert Dahl, of *Politics, Economics and Welfare* (1953).

JOHN LOCKE. 1632–1704. English philosopher. His systematic development of empiricist doctrine and bringing together so many of the important ideas of modern liberalism make him the most influential political philosopher of the Anglo-American political tradition of personal freedom and self-government. Author of *An Essay Concerning Human Understanding* (1690) and *Two Treatises of Civil Government* (1690).

JAMES MADISON. 1751–1836. Fourth president of the United States (1809–1817). His defense of a political system which protects individual freedom and the unequal acquisition of property, ideas on limited government, and contribution to American constitutionalism make his thought very important to Conservatism. Along with Hamilton and Jay he was an author of *The Federalist Papers* (1787–1788).

JOSEPH DE MAISTRE. 1753–1821. French philosopher. His extreme attack on the Enlightenment and the French Revolution make him a leading figure of modern Reactionary thought. Author of *Saint Petersburg Dialogues* (1821).

KARL MANNHEIM. 1893–1947. German sociologist. Pioneer in sociology of knowledge. Author of *Ideology and Utopia* (1936).

JACQUES MARITAIN. 1882–1973. French philosopher. This Catholic intellectual's defense of the Thomistic tradition of thought makes him much admired by Conservatives. Author of *True Humanism* (1938).

KARL MARX. 1818–1883. German political philosopher. Father of modern Communism. Author of *Das Kapital* (3 vols., 1867, 1885, 1895) and with Engels of *The Communist Manifesto* (1848).

FRANK S. MEYER. 1909–1972. Influential American Conservative. His thinking represents the attempt to reconcile the traditionalist and libertarian elements of Conservative thought. Editor of *What Is Conservatism?* (1964).

LUDWIG VON MISES. 1881–1973. Leader of the Austrian school of economics. This important advocate of free-market economics and defender of the traditional liberal conception of individual freedom has influenced many contemporary Conservatives. Author of *Socialism* (1922) and *Human Action* (1949).

THOMAS MOLNAR. 1921– . Hungarian-born educator and author. A defender of traditionalist Conservative values. Author of *Utopia, the Perennial Heresy* (1967).

JUSTUS MÖSER. 1720–1794. German statesman and early Conservative theorist.

GEORGE H. NASH. 1945– . American historian. An authority on the history of contemporary American Conservatism. Author of *The Conservative Intellectual Movement in America Since 1945* (1976).

ROBERT NISBET. 1913– . American sociologist and historian. His studies on community, tradition, and authority have considerable value to contemporary Conservatism. Author of *The Quest for Community* (1953) and *The Sociological Tradition* (1966).

MICHAEL NOVAK. 1933– . American educator, author, and syndicated columnist. An influential defender of religious values and democratic capitalism. Author of *The American Vision* (1978).

MICHAEL OAKESHOTT. 1901– . English philosopher. His critique of rationalism captures the essence of the Conservative's rejection of abstract political thinking. Author of *Experience and Its Modes* (1933) and *Rationalism in Politics and Other Essays* (1962).

JOSÉ ORTEGA Y GASSET. 1883–1955. Spanish philosopher. His attack on mass society and defense of aristocratic values have influenced the Conservative critique of modern society and culture. Author of *Revolt of the Masses* (1930).

STANLEY PARRY. 1918–1972. American clergyman and political thinker. Author of the important essay "Reason and the Restoration of Tradition."

KEVIN PHILLIPS. 1940– . American columnist and author. His critique of liberal elites in the news media, government, and academic community has assisted the development of a neo-populist element within contemporary Conservatism. Author of *The Emerging Republican Majority* (1969).

PLATO. 427?–347 B.C. Famous Greek philosopher. Because of their own disenchantment with much of modern philosophy, many Conservatives have turned to Plato for philosophical inspiration. His classic justification for elite rule and concern for truth, justice, and virtue appeal to many Conservatives. Author of the *Republic.*

NORMAN PODHORETZ. 1930–   . Editor of *Commentary* and an influential neo-Conservative. Author of *Breaking Ranks* (1979).

AYN RAND. 1905–1982. Russian-born author. Her radical individualism influences many libertarians. While many Conservatives admire her critique of modern statism, they are generally critical of her extreme atheism. Author of *Atlas Shrugged* (1957).

JOHN RAWLS. 1921–   . Harvard philosopher. His attempt to breath new life into the social-contract theory involves justifying the basic principles of modern liberalism. Author of *A Theory of Justice* (1971).

RONALD REAGAN. 1911–   . Fortieth president of the United States (1981–   ). Conservatives hope that the election of "one of their own" in 1980 represents an important turning point in American political history.

CLINTON ROSSITER. 1917–1970. American historian. Author of *Conservatism in America* (1955; revised edition, 1962).

JEAN-JACQUES ROUSSEAU. 1712–1778. French political philosopher. One of the most influential thinkers of modern times. Conservatives criticize his theory that man is essentially good but corrupted by society. Author of *Discourse on the Origin of Inequality* (1755) and *The Social Contract* (1762).

ALAN RYAN. 1940–   . English philosopher. Author of *A Philosophy of Social Science* (1971).

JOSEPH SCHUMPETER. 1883–1950. Economic theorist. An influential analyst of modern capitalism and socialism. Author of *Capitalism, Socialism and Democracy* (1942).

B. F. SKINNER. 1904–   . American psychologist. Leading advocate of behaviorism. His ideas are usually attacked by Conservatives. Author of *Beyond Freedom and Dignity* (1971).

ALEKSANDER SOLZHENITSYN. 1918–   . Russian author and political exile. His combined attack on Soviet communism and secular liberalism makes him much admired by Conservatives. Author of many works including *The Gulag Archipelago, 1918–1956* (Part I, 1974; Part II, 1975; Part III, 1976).

BARUCH (BENEDICT) SPINOZA. 1632–1677. Dutch philosopher. One of the greatest rationalistic systems builders of his century. He is generally associated with panthetism. Author of *Ethica Ordine Geometrico Demonstrata* (1674).

PETER J. STANLIS 1920–   . American educator and author. Author of *Edmund Burke and the Natural Law* (1958).

LEO STRAUSS. 1899–1973. Influential teacher and political theorist. His career at The University of Chicago and defense of natural law have had great impact on Conservative thought. Author of *Natural Right and History* (1953).

WILLIAM GRAHAM SUMNER. 1840–1910. American economist and sociologist. He popularized the ideas of Herbert Spencer and social Darwinism in the United States. His defense of laissez-faire liberalism has greatly influenced Conservative economic thinking. Author of *What Social Classes Owe to Each Other* (1883).

MARGARET THATCHER. 1925–   . Prime minister of Great Britain (1979–   ).

THUCYDIDES. 471?–400 B.C. Greek historian. Greatest historian of antiquity. His realistic analysis of war and revolution contains valuable insights for the student of international relations. Author of the *History of the Peloponnesian War*.

ALEXIS DE TOCQUEVILLE. 1805–1859. French political thinker. While generally associated with the liberal tradition of thought, his aristocratic values, concern for personal freedom, fear of majority tyranny, and desire for limited government make him much admired by Conservatives. Author of *Democracy in America* (two volumes, 1835, 1840).

PETER VIERECK. 1916–   . American poet and author. In the 1950s and 60s he stood opposed to those Conservatives who were critical of New Deal liberalism. Author of *Conservatism Revisited and the New Conservatism: What Went Wrong?* (1962).

ERIC VOEGELIN. 1901–   . German-born political philosopher. His critique of positivism and analysis of gnosticism in modern times have had great influence on Conservative thought. Author of *The New Science of Politics* (1952) and *Order and History* (Part I, 1956; Part II, 1957; Part III, 1957; Part IV, 1974; Part V, 1975).

VOLTAIRE. 1694–1778. French philosopher and a leading figure in the Enlightenment. Author of *Candide* (1759).

GEORGE WASHINGTON. 1732–1799. First president of the United States (1789–1797). His prudent leadership, sense of public duty, and patriotism represent essential political virtues stressed by Conservatives.

RICHARD M. WEAVER. 1910–1963. American political theorist. An important defender of traditional Conservative values. Author of *Ideas Have Consequences* (1948).

R. J. WHITE. – . English political thinker. Author of *The Conservative Tradition* (1950).

MAX WEBER. 1864–1920. German sociologist and political theorist. One of the leading sociologists of this century. Criticized by Conservatives because of his positivist methodology. Author of *The Protestant Ethic and the Spirit of Capitalism* (English translation, 1930).

BURLEIGH T. WILKINS. 1932– . American philosopher and educator. Author of *The Problem of Burke's Political Philosophy* (1967).

WOODROW WILSON. 1856–1924. Twenty-eighth president of the United States (1913–1921). His idealistic view of international relations is usually rejected by Conservatives.

Index